DATE DUE

GAYLORD

PRINTED IN U.S.A

D1266000

The Wankel Rotary Engine

The Wankel
Rotary Engine
A History

by
JOHN B. HEGE

McFarland & Company, Inc., Publishers
Jefferson, North Carolina, and London

Library of Congress Cataloguing-in-Publication Data

Hege, John B., 1957–
    The Wankel rotary engine : a history / by John B. Hege
      p.   cm.
    Includes bibliographical references and index.
    ISBN 0-7864-1177-5 (illustrated case binding : 50# alkaline paper) ∞
    1. Automobiles—Motors—History. 2. Wankel engine—History.
  I. Title.
  TL210.7.H44   2002
  621.43'4—dc21   2001052117

British Library cataloguing data are available

Cover photograph: Felix Wankel with the DKM125 prototype of 1957.

Manufactured in the United States of America

McFarland & Company, Inc., Publishers
Box 611, Jefferson, North Carolina 28640
www.mcfarlandpub.com

Acknowledgments

The story of the development of Wankel's rotary engine was told in bits and pieces in the press over a time span of around forty years. Companies made press releases, engineers published papers, and journalists in science and automotive publications gave the public their interpretation. It was through exhaustive reading of all these available materials that I was able to put the story together in something resembling chronological order.

One of the earliest engineer-journalists to be in on the Wankel scene was Jan Norbye, who wrote numerous articles on the Wankel during the sixties and went on to publish a very thorough book on the rotary in 1971. Things were just beginning for the Wankel at that time.

In 1975 Nicholas Faith authored a book that explored the business of bringing the Wankel to market. His work was less technical and focused more on the people who made the Wankel happen.

Max Bentele published several technical papers on rotary engine research while at Curtiss-Wright, and later in his life he published *Engine Revolutions,* an autobiography which tells much of his side of the story of Wankel development.

In the search for illustrations I was able to enlist help from NSU GmbH, which still exists as a business to protect old trademarks and intellectual property of NSU. I also received help from Terry Stuchlik of the NSU Enthusiasts of Alton, Ohio. Mazda Corporation also generously supplied me with illustrations and press release material from their rotary program that I found very helpful. Photographs from Citroën's rotary adventures were supplied by Mme Gro Hoeg of Citroën and from Wouter Jansen, CITROExpert. Photos from the Curtiss-Wright days were supplied by Bill Figart of Rotary Power International, which currently holds all of the Curtiss-Wright rotary technology.

I also want to thank Ernie Lunsford and Vernon Robbins for allowing my son, Jesse Williams, to photograph their cars, and I am also grateful to my son for taking those pictures.

I am thankful too, for my wife and family who encouraged and endured the process of making an author from a crusty old auto mechanic.

Contents

Contents

Introduction

It occurred to me not long ago that I'd grown up with the Wankel engine. I was born in 1957, about the same time that the first example of the Wankel Engine was beginning to sputter to life in a smoke filled research shop at Neckarsulm in West Germany. At that time it was a little known curiosity, another "revolutionary" new configuration for internal combustion. It had, however, attracted enough attention that the development money was there when it was needed. So, in a few years, Felix Wankel and NSU, the small motorcycle company in Germany for which he worked, had a working product that they could present to the public. News about the Wankel showed up in the press just about the time I was old enough to read about it.

That I was a motorhead at a very early age did not go unnoticed by my family. My grandfather, who lived several states away, subscribed to mechanics' magazines and once, during an annual family visit, introduced me to an article about an interesting new "rotary piston" engine which was just attracting the attention of the press. Each summer after that, we would drive to Pennsylvania to visit, and my grandfather and I would discuss the new Wankel developments of the past year. I soaked up as much information as my young age would allow, which turned out to be more than I had realized. In fact, many of the old magazine articles that I read during my later research stirred up vague old memories of reading them as a child and struggling to understand what they meant.

Over the years I absorbed a great deal of history without ever realizing it. Between reading technical journals and working as an auto mechanic, I saw developments come and go. What worked, what did not, what lasted, what failed, what sold, what flopped, all passed under my nose as part of my daily routine. Now I am the old man in a shop staffed mostly by young men for whom the Mazda rotary has always been a part of the automotive world. But even among auto mechanics, men for whom an automobile engine holds no mysteries, there has always been a certain amount of awe and mystique surrounding the Mazda rotaries. Few people besides specialists have ever torn one down for repairs. Standard operating procedure has always been to replace a worn out rotary and ship the old unit off to the factory for rebuilding, so few mechanics outside of a Mazda dealership even know what makes them tick.

Not long ago, I replaced an engine in a 1986 RX-7 and intercepted the junk engine before it went to the rebuilders. I tore it down for the other mechanics to inspect it and to answer some questions about its basic construction. We were all taken by the beauty of its geometry and the elegance of its motion. I was called on to answer questions about Wankel history. Being well on my way to becoming a boring old man, I felt compelled to throw in little known tidbits such as "You know, Rolls-Royce once built a diesel Wankel," or "The British were building Wankel powered motorcycles as late as 1987."

While everyone else rolled their eyes, I just became more curious, but when I tried to find some more reading material on the subject, all I found were disjointed articles. Eventually I found out-of-print histories that stopped short of the late seventies, which was a very important time in the life span of the Wankel. I could not find any comprehensive work following the Wankel engine from its beginnings to the present. So I thought I would take the information that I had gathered and do one myself.

As it turns out, it is a fascinating story. After about ten years of development, major auto manufacturers were being forced to acknowledge the virtues of Wankel's new engine. One after another, the early problems with the engine were being solved and many of the early skeptics were converted. Development was facilitated by unique patent licensing agreements, which called for sharing of technology among many of the licensees. Excessive oil consumption, smoking and high emission levels were all sorted out and some of the more daring manufacturers were producing rotary powered cars that were performing well in real-world conditions. Even the huge and ultimately conservative American auto manufacturers were building prototypes and hinting at plans to convert several of their car lines to rotary power.

For a time the whole world appeared ready to go rotary. Investors were trying to interpret clues as to what the major manufacturers were up to. If General Motors made a big real-estate purchase, there would be speculation that it was for their new rotary engine factory. The stocks of companies holding pieces of Wankel technology were climbing. Major auto executives were publicly predicting, "In ten years, the entire auto industry will be 95 percent rotary." Then, because of political events, which may or may not have been predictable, the bottom suddenly fell out, catching many rotary proponents off guard. Only Mazda, which had so much invested in the rotary that it could not back out, continued to show any interest in future automotive rotary markets. Other companies in small corners of the world were quietly producing rotaries, but their small output amounted to little more than dabbling.

Mazda bet what they had on the rotary and almost lost big. The company nearly caved in as sales dropped off by half, then half again. They cautiously diversified their car line to include more conventional vehicles. But they hung on to the rotary, worked on their product, and were able to continue to build successful cars marketed on the basis of the rotary's unique performance properties for twenty years.

It has been said that the automotive industry is given to evolution, not revolution. Rarely do new ideas have enough impact to get the attention of anyone but a few technocrats behind the scenes. The machinery behind the status quo is far too large and cumbersome to be changed for any reason other than a sure thing. An invention that does not promise huge financial success usually disappears quietly into the warehouses of the research and development laboratories. Ideas may be studied and developed, and they may even be adopted, but not in such a fashion that the car owner might notice. "Assimilated" would probably be a more apt description. They eventually become part of the technology that powers the same old stroker. But Felix Wankel's revolutionary new engine got enough attention, if only for a few years, to threaten to alter the entire automotive industry forever.

1

Why a Rotary?

If reciprocating engines had started out being as efficient and reliable as they are today, no one might have searched for an alternative design. But during the early decades of development, the reciprocating internal combustion engine seemed inherently flawed. Quite a few engineering hurdles remained to be overcome, and a great deal of experimentation was taking place. Many inventors advocated throwing the whole package out, in favor of a new layout. After all, at the time there was no conventional wisdom to indicate that a gasoline engine had to be built in any one particular fashion. Certainly nobody could be sure that Otto's reciprocating four-stroke would be embraced by the entire world and be developed as thoroughly as it has been. The industrial world seemed reasonably open to new ideas about how to capture the expansion energy of burning fuels and convert it into circular motion.

In the second half of the nineteenth century, inventors had studied internal combustion as a replacement for steam. Like a steam engine, a reciprocating internal combustion engine uses the pressure of expanding gas to move a piston through a cylinder, the piston being linked to a crankshaft by a connecting rod to convert its back-and-forth movement into a much more useful circular motion. But to drive a steam engine, you have to produce steam in an external boiler. Being large and heavy, and given to occasional explosions, boilers of the nineteenth century were not considered practical for use in small vehicles. Their place seemed to be in large installations, ships and trains, or as stationary engines for powering factory equipment. Numerous companies developed steam powered autos, but most of the world viewed internal combustion as the way to make a truly compact powerplant.

The man credited with producing the first really useful internal combustion engine is Nicholas Augustus Otto. Otto worked in a machine shop during the 1860s, a time of strong interest in new engines of any kind. He made several attempts at constructing engines but really made a hit working with Eugene Langen, another engineer. They built a stationary piston engine which won for them a gold award at the Paris World Exhibition in 1867. This was not the famous Otto four-stroke—it was more similar in fact to a two-cycle engine—but it was a working internal combustion engine which Otto could produce for sale and around which he built a small manufacturing company.

After manufacturing stationary engines for several years, he took another look at a scheme he had tried years before but abandoned. This arrangement broke the operation of the engine down into four distinct cycles. Each cycle took place in one sweep of the piston, and valves were used to admit, contain, and exhaust the combustion gases. He patented the engine in 1877 and began production of the "Otto Silent Engine," the principle of which would turn out to be the foundation of the automotive industry to come.[1]

The process begins with the intake stroke. The piston is descending in the cylinder and the intake valve is open. The fuel-air mixture is drawn into the cylinder in pump-like fashion as the crankshaft rotates 180 degrees (Fig. 1). Reaching the bottom of its stroke, the piston reverses direction and the intake valve closes. The piston sweeps upward, compressing the inhaled gases to a fraction of their original volume (Fig. 2). At the point of maximum compression the mixture is ignited, usually by electric spark, and the piston is driven downward by the force of the expanding gases (Fig. 3). The crankshaft continues to turn, the exhaust valve opens, and the spent gases are forced out by the pumping action of the piston traveling upward (Fig. 4).

Engines built on Otto's "four stroke" principle were much more powerful for their size than their more primitive ancestors, so it became possible to propel carriage- and wagon-sized vehicles with small gasoline engines. The concept was quickly embraced around the world and inventors and engineers began tinkering with and developing different engine layouts. The automobile industry was born in several parts of the world as pioneers like Carl Benz and Charles and Frank Duryea began marketing their gasoline powered cars using engines developed around Otto's four-stroke principle. Engines became more powerful and reliable, but they still failed frequently—and their failures

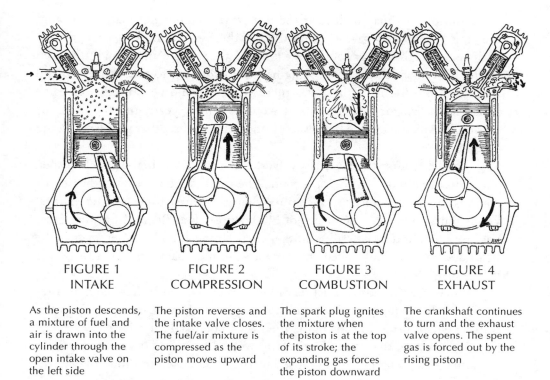

| FIGURE 1 | FIGURE 2 | FIGURE 3 | FIGURE 4 |
| INTAKE | COMPRESSION | COMBUSTION | EXHAUST |

As the piston descends, a mixture of fuel and air is drawn into the cylinder through the open intake valve on the left side

The piston reverses and the intake valve closes. The fuel/air mixture is compressed as the piston moves upward

The spark plug ignites the mixture when the piston is at the top of its stroke; the expanding gas forces the piston downward

The crankshaft continues to turn and the exhaust valve opens. The spent gas is forced out by the rising piston

Figures 1–4. The four-stroke cycle.

were often catastrophic. If a small internal part like a connecting rod bolt failed, an engine could quickly be reduced to junk, testifying to the tremendous forces which must be handled inside a working engine. Building an engine that would produce any kind of useful power meant stretching the limits of materials and design, and as the power went up, the destructive forces inside the engine necessarily would rise, and reliability would go down.

It was the wide variety of motion inside a gasoline engine that troubled early inventors. To begin with, a piston had to be stopped, reversed, and restarted four times for each power cycle. In a medium sized automobile engine under ordinary driving conditions, it might accelerate to 300 feet per second and then decelerate to zero in the space of about three inches. The stresses of this motion often led to failures of the pistons themselves and of the wrist pins and connecting rods which linked them to the crankshaft. At the top of the pistons, the sealing rings have to endure the stress and heat of combustion and be forced against either side of their groove each time the piston reverses direction. Under certain conditions such as pre-ignition, or spark-knock, rings and pistons may melt near the top, or the supporting material around the ring groove may give way, destroying the piston, and consequently the entire engine. To further complicate matters, there is the vibration introduced by the heavy connecting rods swinging back and forth to the piston's up and down motion. Many of these destructive forces could be cancelled or compensated for by good design, but it would be many years into the development of the piston engine before solutions to these and other problems would be found.

Then of course there are the valves. Their job is a brutal one: They open and close hundreds of times a second. The intakes are alternately heated by combustion then cooled by incoming charge with each cycle. The exhaust valves must endure temperatures of 1400 degrees F as the still-burning gases pass by them and must still maintain their strength and temper so that the head does not snap off when the valve is slammed back onto its seat by the valve spring.

Of course the valves must be driven somehow, and it must be done precisely. So this requires a whole additional system of cams, lifters, springs and rockers which bring to the engine their own potential for failure.

It's amazing that it can be made to work. But it can. It works so well, in fact, that piston engines are produced by the hundreds of millions all over the world. But there always has been room for improvement. Many of the engineers and inventors in the first half of the century who cared about such things were sure that the key to reliability and longevity in an engine was to do away with the wasted motion. They saw all this metal flailing about in order to rotate a shaft and figured that there had to be a better way.

Periodically, the automotive world would see a new type of gasoline engine. It would usually be called a rotary to describe the theme of continuous circular motion. Most were derivations of existing pump configurations. Many of them worked, but most had problems with combustion sealing. Machinery that worked well for moving and compressing gases didn't hold up as well to the heat, pressure and by-products of combustion. Some were too difficult or expensive to manufacture. A piston engine's greatest redeeming quality turned out to be that all of its sliding and sealing surfaces could be made by boring holes or turning parts on a lathe. Sealing the combustion pressure, an important part of engine longevity and efficiency, is more easily done with a circular shape, and round holes are cheaper to manufacture than the often bizarre shapes required by rotary designs. So most rotaries just came and went. Some attracted more attention than others, but few ever saw much development or made it into mass-production.

Intake valves are alternately heated by combustion and cooled by incoming charge with each power cycle. They must be made of materials that can withstand the thermal loading.

Valves require complex drive systems to operate them in perfect synchronization with the crankshaft. The valve drive can add hundreds of parts to an engine.

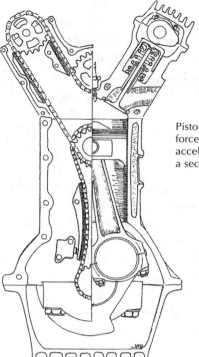

Exhaust valves operate at temperatures just short of burning. Incorrect fuel mixture, leakage, and excessive loads can lead to burning and breakage.

Pistons are subjected to tremendous force as they stop, reverse, and accelerate about one hundred times a second during normal driving.

Connecting rods have a very complex motion in which the upper part moves up and down, while the lower part follows a circular path. The forces contained in this motion are sometimes enough to tear the connecting rod apart under high loads.

Figure 5. Points of stress in a conventional reciprocating engine.

When Felix Wankel's new "rotary piston" engine first started appearing in popular technical journals in 1960, it was not a particularly surprising announcement. After all, inventors had been producing their alternatives to reciprocating pistons for years. What was surprising was the attention that it received in the industry. There must have been something a little more substantial to the claims its proponents made, claims that had been heard many times before.

First of all, the Wankel engine was unusually small for its power output. Compared to a piston engine of similar displacement, the basic engine was only about half as large. This stimulated the imaginations of automobile designers who loved to dream about ultra-low hood lines, mid-engine configurations, and front or four wheel drive cars which were not yet in fashion. The engine was small enough to fit almost anywhere.

The simple construction of the engine seemed to lend itself well to building small engines. It seemed to be a good potential competitor for two-stroke engines for powering chain saws, lawn equipment, and outboard motors. Yet the design also appeared well suited for large applications, and some companies were talking about modular construction, stacking up additional rotors to produce engines of larger displacement. By the time they presented the engine publicly, Curtiss-Wright, a major American aircraft manufacturing company that had bought a large stake in the Wankel, was experimenting with multi-rotor engines stacked in tandem.

The engineers were very excited about the lack of vibration; that was what the rotary was all about, wasn't it? Wankel and other inventors had worked on the rotary concept for years because they couldn't be comfortable with all those different pieces of a reciprocating engine moving back and forth. Wankel's engine eliminated that; at all times during operation, all the pieces in a Wankel engine continued to revolve in the same direction. There was no stopping and starting, no reversing direction, just a smooth whirling. The engine ran practically vibration free, and engineers were convinced that this would contribute to the longevity and reliability of any machine that was powered by a rotary engine.

Proponents also felt that the engine would, in the long run, be cheaper to produce. This was an arguable point because of the unusual shapes involved in the construction of the rotors and chambers. Of course, circles were easier to manufacture and few people outside of the mathematics community had ever heard of an epitrochoid, which was the term used to describe the shape of the housings. But NSU engineers said that once the initial tooling was done, the engine was very inexpensive to produce because of its small number of parts.

Another advantage of the Wankel, which showed up in testing and early development, was its resistance to spark-knock. (Spark-knock, or pre-ignition, is a destructive problem that occurs in piston engines usually due to hot spots in the combustion chambers, use of inferior grade fuel, or both.) In some high power designs, extremely high-grade gasoline was needed to control pre-ignition in traditional reciprocating engines. This was sometimes costly and was unavailable in certain parts of the world. Even though it had an ordinary compression ratio of 8.5 to 1, the Wankel would run well on very low-grade fuel.

Most of these claims didn't sound particularly new, but they drew a lot of favorable attention. Felix Wankel's employer, NSU, was only a small motorcycle manufacturer and lacked the financial wherewithal to fully develop and exploit their new toy. They looked for a major partner to help them get the most out of Wankel's invention, finding one in Curtiss-Wright in 1958. A major aircraft manufacturer, Curtiss-Wright announced that it had purchased a license to develop and produce Wankel engines of all sizes in the United States for $2.1 million. The agreement also permitted them to sell licenses for producing Wankel engines to other companies. This agreement turned a few heads in the automotive industry. Maybe there was more to this new engine than there was to some of the earlier ideas. A few of the industry minds thought it would be prudent to take a closer look.

How the Wankel Works

The Wankel reproduces the four cycles of the Otto engine using an almost-triangular (trochoidal) rotor moving around in an almost-elliptical (epitrochoidal) housing. Understanding the motion of the rotor in the housing is the key to understanding the operation of the engine. The three tips of the rotor are kept in contact with the sides of the housing throughout the whole cycle of the rotor. The tips are fitted with seals to divide one space from the other. The small gear illustrated in Figs. 6–9 does not move, but is fixed to one side of the rotor housing. The larger gear is fitted to one side of the rotor. The rotor whirls around the small gear like a hula-hoop; the teeth are there only to keep it in phase. In the other side of the rotor is fitted a plain babbitt style bearing which allows the rotor to turn on an eccentric shaft. The eccentric shaft passes through the center of the small gear and serves as the output shaft. The eccentric shaft turns three revolutions for every single revolution of the rotor.

The combination of the eccentric shaft and the "timing" or "phasing" gear causes the rotor to move around the housing with the tips following a path called an epitrochoid, which, while being fairly complex mathematically, looks like a sort of oval with a pinched center. This path that the rotor tips follow forms three separate chambers whose volume is constantly changing, which makes it useful as an engine or pump design. Each of the three chambers is undergoing a different part of the four-stroke Otto Cycle at any given time. In the first drawing (Fig. 6), chamber A is in its intake cycle as the chamber is open to the intake port and the mixture is being drawn into the engine. Chamber B is at maximum compression and is being ignited. Chamber C is open to the exhaust port and is beginning its exhaust phase. In the next drawing, (Fig. 7), the eccentric shaft has turned 90 degrees, but the rotor has only moved 30. Chamber A is at the maximum point of the intake cycle, just before the port closes. Chamber B is in the power cycle, being driven by the combustion gases. And chamber C is well into exhaust as the moving

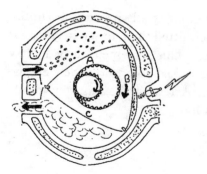

FIGURE 6

Each of the three faces of the rotor is undergoing a different phase of a four-cycle engine. In this illustration, side A is open to the intake port and is drawing in fresh mixture. Side B is at maximum compression and is being ignited. Side C has just opened the exhaust port.

FIGURE 7

Now side A is at peak volume and the intake port is about to close. Side B is being driven by combustion, and side C is forcing out the spent exhaust gas.

FIGURE 8

The intake port has now closed on side A and compression is beginning. Side B has nearly reached the end of the expansion cycle, and side C has finished exhausting and is beginning a new intake cycle.

FIGURE 9

Here side A is approaching maximum compression. Side B has opened to the exhaust port, and side C is continuing its intake stroke. By the time the eccentric shaft has moved through 360° of rotation, the rotor will only have moved 120°.

Figures 6–9. The Wankel cycle.

rotor drives the spent gas out through the port. In Figure 8 the rotor has moved another 30 degrees and the shaft another 90. Chamber A is beginning compression, chamber B is ending its power stroke as the opening of the exhaust port approaches, and chamber C has completed exhaust and is about to start its intake phase. In figure 9, again the shaft has moved 90 degrees more and the rotor another 30. Chamber A is approaching maximum compression. Chamber B has just begun its exhaust. And chamber C is thirty degrees into its intake phase.

Looking back at a single cylinder Otto engine, it can be seen that only one fourth of the period of crankshaft rotation is used to produce power. For every two revolutions of the crankshaft, only one half of one revolution is spent under power. The rest of the time the crankshaft is coasting around using the inertia of its flywheel to keep it going.

In the Wankel, there are three working faces on the rotor. When one side is producing power, one side is on intake stroke, and one side is on exhaust. The rotor is being driven through a much larger portion of its period of rotation. As the output shaft (eccentric) is driven at three times the rotor speed, and the rotor has three firing pulses per revolution, this becomes one firing stroke per revolution at the flywheel. To achieve this with a piston would require two cylinders. This explains why the Wankel is such a compact powerplant.

Because the rotor is always traveling in the same direction, there is little vibration to the engine. There is a small counterweight fixed to the eccentric to smooth out some of the wobble from the rotor, but compared to a piston engine, the Wankel is practically vibration free. Piston engines are full of parts that must stop and start, change direction, and rock back and forth which shake the engine in every conceivable direction. Large counterweights are often added, and sometimes even complex systems of counterweighted balance shafts are installed, but even then, a certain amount of vibration is accepted as being inevitable.

Another noteworthy feature of the Wankel is the absence of valves. Because the working chamber in the engine is constantly in motion, the function of intake and exhaust can be performed by having the rotor pass over ports in the housing. In this way the Wankel can be compared to a two-cycle engine. Experiments with "valve" timing can be done by altering the shape and the location of the ports. Elimination of the valve drive system can save the production of hundreds of parts per engine in some cases.

Early on, Wankel's engine suffered from many of the same problems that kept other designs from succeeding. Sealing combustion chamber pressures from one chamber to the other was a continuous headache for every company that became involved with the Wankel. The first engines smoked copiously and consumed huge amounts of oil right up until the time that they would self-destruct after a few hours on the test stand. Initial tooling for machining the epitrochoidal chambers was formidably expensive. Materials science was only just emerging, and the development of new alloys and new casting and coating methods would be very important in the story of the engine. But there is an elegance to the Wankel that is unique. Seeing it on paper, one can try to visualize the intricate, interlinked circles that come together to make it work. Handling the pieces and working them through their motion inspires simultaneous thoughts of "Of course!" and "But how?" Maybe it was this elegance that attracted the right kind of attention from investors to see that the Wankel Rotary went much farther than its ill-fated brethren.

2

Early Experiments

Long before Felix Wankel's death in 1988, the work of his lifetime had shaken up the industrial world in a way that few others ever would. To build a new engine that can tempt the entire world automotive industry to convert to another source of power is no small feat. Revolutionary inventions come and go along with their inventors, but Wankel was clever enough and fortunate enough to be involved with the right people to see his engine through its critical gestation period, men who were less inclined to look at the balance sheet than they were to study a unique new engine and see opportunity beyond the end-of-the year profit reports. To make the necessary commitment to develop an entirely new power plant took guts, especially for the leaders of the smaller companies that started out with the Wankel. At any time, the bottom could have fallen out—and sometimes it did, taking careers and reputations with it. But a few engineers, executives and investors saw the Wankel engine as an inspired concept and were committed to seeing it through. Wankel himself was mostly self-educated as an engineer and had little formal education beyond high school, but he was eventually awarded an honorary professorship for his groundbreaking work in rotary engines.

Engineers are born. Mechanical minds are just wired that way from the start. Although less mechanical types can be well trained, there is a type of mind that instinctively understands machinery, a mind that has an intensity of focus and an unusual ability to visualize three-dimensional objects. It can turn a shape around, picturing it from different angles. The same way some people can perform complex mathematical operations without ever setting pencil to paper, a natural engineer can visualize machine components moving in harmony without ever having seen the machines themselves. For these people, studying mechanical structures and motion and trying to understand mechanisms comes as naturally as eating or sleeping. They can't help but look for flaws in a device and imagine ways in which it could be improved, and they are as likely to do it on the walk home as while in the workshop. Or they may take a small feature of one device and add it to another to produce a third that resembles neither parent in form or function. All this they may do for their own amusement as much as for any possibility of any financial success.

The beginning of the twentieth century was a fertile time for such a person, as there were a great many machines offering opportunities for improvement. Gasoline engines and other things mechanical were in a very crude state and there was much work to be done in development. But they were easy to understand to the right type of mind, and even if a person had little or no formal education, the workings of a gasoline engine had not become such a science that they could not be mastered intuitively.

Felix Heinrich Wankel was a natural engineer, but was not born into an environment likely to nurture such an inclination. In 1902 he was born in the village of Lahr in southwestern Germany, a place where he would be more likely to go into farming, like most of the town, or forest management, like his father, Rudolf.

His father was killed early in the First World War when Wankel was only 12. But Wankel was fortunate to be able to continue to attend school until he graduated in 1921. To go to another town and become a machinist's apprentice or something similar would probably have been an appropriate move at the time for a young man of his bent, but Wankel had to earn a living for himself and his widowed mother, so he took a job instead in Heidelburg as a salesman of school books for a publishing company. A large part of his natural talent was in mechanical drawing, and on his own time he was always studying new ways of approaching old mechanical problems, producing drawings describing rotary valve systems and purely theoretical machines that, given the time and money, he would build. In 1924 he opened a mechanical workshop in Heidelburg, giving himself a better outlet than the home shop for his need to work among things mechanical.

Wankel was among those who saw the piston engines of the time as a nightmare of conflicting motions. Very early in his career he made drawings and spoke of his desire to build a pure-rotary internal-combustion engine.

While much of his mechanical work took him in other directions, the rotary engine idea was one that would simply not go away. It is a complicated problem, accomplishing everything that Otto did with his four-stroke piston engine in a rotating chamber. Several pump-like designs could be adapted, but the issue of sealing kept coming up. Containing the heat and pressure of combusting gases between two sliding metal surfaces was an infant science, and a necessary one for the purpose of building any type of internal combustion engine. Wankel studied the issue relentlessly throughout his career. Sealing high pressures inside moving machinery became his field as it had many commercial applications beyond its necessity in everything that he wanted to do.

Much of Wankel's early work was devoted to developing an alternative for the poppet style valve that was popular during the 1920s and 1930s in gasoline engines, but was not yet universal as it is today. While the modern design is little changed from the twenties, the metals used in its construction have advanced greatly, making it a fairly reliable part in most cases. But in the 1920s, the valve was made of mild steel and, being prone to burn around the edges and break off into the cylinder, was considered a sorely weak spot in a four-cycle engine. Several working engines in production used sleeve valves, and some manufacturers wanted to experiment with disk valves. Seeing rotary disk valves as a logical step toward a rotary engine development, Wankel started experimenting by modifying motorcycle engines with different designs. In the course of these experiments, he encountered many of the same types of sealing problems that he would experience later on in development of his rotary engine, and he developed and patented several systems to cope with those problems.

Piston rings had already been around for a long time, and their effectiveness at sealing high pressures on one side of a moving piston was universally accepted. It was obvious that the pressure of combustion could not be contained behind a piston that had enough clearance within its cylinder to move freely. The sealing rings were added as movable elements held against the cylinder wall by spring tension and gas pressure. The free movement allows the rings to expand and contract according to the temperature and to follow the irregularities in the cylinder wall brought on by wear, thus providing a pressure chamber in which to contain the combustion gases.

At first glance, the job of the sealing rings seems simple. But a closer look reveals the role that they play in production of power. The combustion gases that flow around the top of the piston force the ring down against the bottom of its groove. A portion of the gases, the amount of which is controlled by design, enters the space behind the ring and forces the ring more tightly

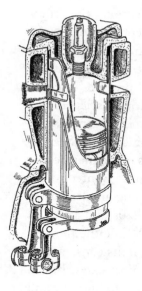

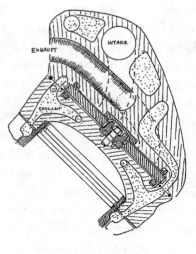

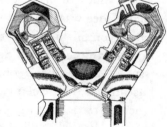

Above: Poppet style valves eventually won the contest and became the universal automotive engine valve. The valves themselves are simple, though the drive systems often are not. Because the valve is stationary during the high-pressure phase of operation, it can provide a perfect seal.

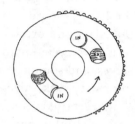

Sleeve valve engines were known for their quiet operation, but among their drawbacks were high oil consumption and short life between overhauls because of sealing problems between the movable sleeves

Above and right: Wankel's disk valve cylinder heads had a single disk atop each cylinder. The disks were geared on their perimeter so that each disk drove the disk next to it.. By replacing the bulky valve train with a series of disks, a V-8 engine was made small enough to fit inside a torpedo.

Figure 10. Sleeve, disk and poppet valves.

against the cylinder. The piston is thrust downward in the cylinder, mostly by the pressure against its crown, but also by the pressure of the piston ring against the lower surface of its groove. The ring spends most of its time forced against the bottom of the groove, kept there by the pressure of combustion, compression, and exhaust. But for one stroke, it shuffles to the top surface of the groove as the pressure in the cylinder reverses, to draw in the intake charge.

The rings also play an important part in heat transfer. If a piston has nowhere to send its heat, the temperature will build up until the piston melts or burns. Some of the heat is given up to the oil where it splashes on the underside of the piston crown. But most of the heat must be transferred to the cylinder walls where it can be carried away by the cooling system medium. The piston skirts can carry some, but their contact with the cylinder walls is not positive because of the working clearance and the movement of the piston. The rings can provide an effective transfer path for heat to the cylinder because of their positive contact with the piston and the cylinder wall.

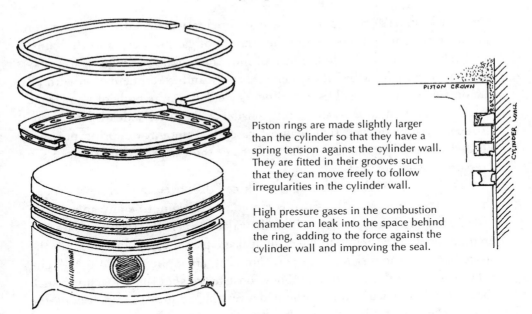

Piston rings are made slightly larger than the cylinder so that they have a spring tension against the cylinder wall. They are fitted in their grooves such that they can move freely to follow irregularities in the cylinder wall.

High pressure gases in the combustion chamber can leak into the space behind the ring, adding to the force against the cylinder wall and improving the seal.

Figure 11. Leakage problems with piston rings.

The subtleties of piston ring design were still being discovered at the time but nobody understood them better than Wankel. He had learned a great deal about cylinder sealing during his own experiments and was trying to apply what he had learned to his disk valve designs. The problem of sealing gas in a chamber against sliding surfaces was the same, but the shapes were not. Circles have always been easier to drill, plug or seal than straight lines or irregular shapes, and Wankel's challenge was to apply piston ring principles to straight lines and irregular shapes.

Experiments with disk valves involved spring loaded "packing bodies" to do the job of sealing. The piece that Wankel referred to as a packing body was like a piston ring in function if not also in form. This was the element which would ride in a machined groove, spring loaded with its machined face presses against the sliding surface. If the concept was simple enough the practice was not. The difficulty arose in finding the right balance between spring pressure and gas pressure against the bottom of the packing body, and the thickness and surface area of the face. If the spring pressure were too high, rapid wear of the seal would result. If it were too low, the seal would be compromised. Too much gas pressure also caused rapid wear. A wide seal with a large surface area would distribute the load some, but thermal loads could then result in a warped sealing surface, reducing the effectiveness of the seal.

Some of Wankel's arrangements for experimentation included provision for adjusting the spring pressure and the amount of gas allowed to work against the back of the seal. While the idea of moveable metal sealing surfaces may not have been new, Wankel's systematic study and experimentation with all the details involved was. His experiments yielded a large body of knowledge of which shapes, materials, and spring tension worked best under different conditions. Results showed that in most cases the amount of spring pressure needed was really quite low with the force of the gas producing most of the pressure needed for sealing.

Disk valves work by passing a machined disk over an open port. When the port is covered and the valve is closed, there cannot be any appreciable leakage between the surfaces. When the valve is open and the port is uncovered, it is still undesirable to have any leakage past the opening and into the space between the disk and the port. For such an application, Wankel's circular seals were relatively simple. They consisted of split rings, machined such that one side was flat and the other side was shaped into a ramp, leaving the ring thicker in profile on one side than the other. The rings were pinned together to prevent relative movement with the ramps facing each other. With the seal installed, the spring force against the surfaces was provided by the two rings expanding against each other.

Because the ports were not always round, Wankel developed other means of closing the gaps. For rectangular or otherwise irregular openings, he fashioned metal strips that would lie, inter-linked with cylindrical joint components. Using this system he could build an uninterrupted sealing system around virtually any shaped port. This system would show up years later on his engines.

Wankel patented his first rotary engine in 1934. It was a true rotary, a "concentric" engine in his terminology, but it lacked the simplicity of his later design. Its operation is as difficult to describe as it is to understand. The engine had two rotors and counter-rotors. The rotors were rectangular in section and ran in circular chambers. The lower rotor and its counter-rotor performed the intake and compression cycles and the upper rotor and counter-rotor performed combustion and exhaust.

The circular chambers in which the rotors and counter-rotors ran were interlinked to form a sort of figure eight. Each rotor and its counter were geared such that their leading and trailing edges could pass closely, but not touch. They rotated in opposite directions so that their motion resembled a pair of one-toothed gears. When the compressor rotor passed over the intake port, and the port was open, the fuel mixture was drawn in as the trailing edge

SLIDING SURFACE   DISK SURFACE

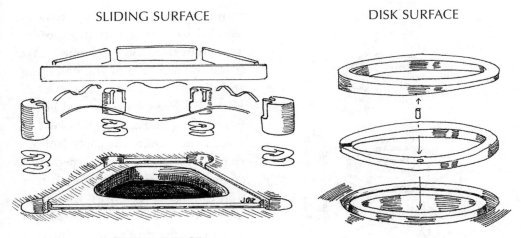

PORT SURFACE   PORT SURFACE

Figure 12, *left.* **Wankel's packing body seals were similar to piston rings in that they were made of movable parts fitted into finely machined grooves. A network of strips connected by peg-like trunnions enabled him to seal any shape of opening against a moving surface. Wankel's seals also provide for a certain amount of gas leakage behind the sealing elements. Figure 13,** *right.* **For sealing ports in disk valve systems, Wankel used two rings, stacked one on the other. Having a ramp-like profile at complementary angles, they were pinned loosely together, to prevent their rotating. When the gas pressure is high, and sealing is needed most, gas leaks in between the rings and forces the supper one against the disk, making a gas-tight seal.**

of the rotor retreated from the hole. Eventually, the intake port was shut off by the front edge of the rotor and the fuel mixture was carried around the chamber, until it encountered the outer side of the counter-rotor. The compressor rotor continued to turn, compressing the mixture between the leading edge of the compressor rotor and the back side of the counter-rotor. At maximum compression, the port was uncovered that communicated with the upper chamber and the compressed mixture was sent upstairs to be burned. In the upper chamber, the fuel was lit as soon as the common port was covered. The power rotor was driven around by pressure until the exhaust was allowed to exit through a port in the counter-rotor's housing.

The concentric engine worked, but it was disappointing in several ways. It was too complicated and difficult to machine. It was too bulky and too heavy for its power output. But it served well as a proving ground for some of Wankel's ideas on sealing straight lines and irregular openings.

The year 1933 was not an easy time to be a German. Even a person in such an apparently apolitical trade as a machinist stood a good chance of

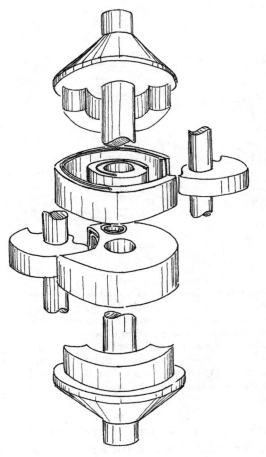

Figure 14. Wankel's concentric engine patented in 1934.

running afoul of the politicians. Wankel had taken part in exposing an embezzlement scheme that involved members of the emerging socialist (Nazi) party. When Adolf Hitler became chancellor and began imprisoning his enemies, Wankel was jailed as a traitor to the party. But the respect that Wankel had earned as an engineer and machinist had left him well connected. His work with sealing solutions and rotary valves had given him the experience he needed to become a sought-after expert in the field. Daimler-Benz took an interest in his work and Dr. Otto Nibel, Daimler-Benz's chief engineer, contacted Wilhelm Keppler, who was acting as one of Hitler's advisors. Keppler, who had already met Wankel several years earlier, had sufficient leverage to have him released, and Wankel went to work for Mercedes-Benz. It was the first of a series of favors that Keppler would do for Wankel.

Wankel's employment at Mercedes-Benz ended after quarrels with the general manager in less than a year. Wankel left the company to work for BMW doing much the same kind of work developing a piston engine with rotary disk valves.

By 1936 the government had been alerted to his reputation as an engineer and he was sought out by the air ministry of Hermann Goering. He was asked to bring his work to Berlin, but Wankel didn't want to live in Berlin. With Keppler's help, he instead was able to persuade Goering to set up shop for him in Lindau on Lake Constance. The government built him a large facility there, expecting him to build a rotary disk valve aircraft engine.

The engine that he produced was a modified Daimler-Benz DB601 V-12, a 33.4 liter, inverted vee, liquid cooled, twelve cylinder. Wankel's disk valves covered the top of the cylinder bore. The outer periphery of each disk was cut as a gear, each disk driving the one next to it. They were driven by a pinion gear off of the crankshaft at one-fourth engine speed. Each disk had two openings that would pass over circular exhaust and intake ports. The ports were fitted with a two piece split ring seal patented by Wankel earlier. The outer periphery was sealed by a piston ring sort of affair set into a groove in the head. Combustion pressure was allowed to work on both sides of the disk, keeping it from being it forced too hard against the sealing elements of one side or the other. After extensive testing, the disk-valve DB601 went into production to be installed in fighter planes for the Luftwaffe.

Probably the greatest advantage of a disk valve engine is its size and relative simplicity. By arranging the disks to drive one another, as Wankel did, valve stems, valve springs, rocker arms, lifters and camshafts can all be eliminated. On most engines, this takes quite a bit off of the top, making a V-8 engine small enough even to fit inside a torpedo. That would be where many Wankel designed disk valves would end up.

The requirements for a torpedo engine are similar to the requirements for a drag racer. It has to come up to speed quickly and run at full output for only a short period of time. Long-term wear is less important since the engine will simply be blown up before it shuts down. But the engine had some design features added in later years meant to extend the life of the disk valves. Pressure lubricated thrust bearings were placed above the disks to help them endure the high loads placed on them by combustion. Needle bearings were used at the center of the disks, and the cylinder head had cooling jackets above and below the cavity where the disk ran in hopes of preventing distortion of the disk due to overheating.

It was during Wankel's work on the KM8 that the Second World War came to an end. After the end, Wankel wound up in prison again, this time as a Nazi scientist. Upon his release in 1946, he was forbidden from doing any practical research or experimental work. So he spent the next few years doing academic work, studying, writing, and sketching out designs for the ultimate rotary engine that he still wanted to build. Eventually he opened another workshop in Lindau near the site of his old facility. His old friend Wilhelm Keppler, after freeing himself of his own post-war political burdens, helped Wankel obtain contracts with other companies in the re-emerging German machine industry. His most important contract for the future came from a chance meeting between Keppler and an NSU executive as they had adjacent hospital beds for a time while they were both recovering from an illness. Keppler mentioned that he knew a man who had developed a rotary valve that his company might be able to use on their motorcycle engines. This casual conversation found its way back to the company and eventually led to the association between Wankel and NSU, the association that would provide the venue and most of the funds to make his rotary engine a reality.

3

Wankel at NSU

NSU was a small motorcycle company that had somehow survived much of the Allied bombing raids of the war. It was one of the older companies in Europe, having been originally a maker of automated knitting machinery. The initials NSU stand for Neckarsulm Strickmachinen Union, or Neckarsulm Knitting Machine Company. The chief executive, Gerd Steiler von Heydekampf, had been the manager of Opel, the German branch of General Motors, before the war. In spite of his obvious qualifications, he was not able to take control of NSU directly because of the burden of his past: During the war, he had run a company that produced tanks and locomotives. After having difficulty finding a position of responsibility in postwar Germany, he was allowed to take a job as a salesman for NSU, from which position he became chief executive in a few short years.

Two other men responsible for bringing Wankel to NSU were Dr. Victor Frankenberger and Dr. Walter Froede. Frankenberger was in charge of the production and technical side of the company, and Froede was the chief engineer. Having heard of Wankel and his work through the hospital conversation, Frankenberger contacted him in Lindau and asked him to come to Nekarsulm to talk about a possible research contract, but Wankel insisted that they send someone to see him instead. So Walter Froede, the chief engineer of NSU went to visit Wankel on his own turf. Wankel showed Froede many of his designs and reports, and spoke of his intention to build a rotary engine.

25

He almost got carried away as he waxed prophetic about rotary powered personal watercraft that could cross the oceans like automobiles on a highway. Froede was impressed with much of Wankel's work, and said so when he returned to Neckarsulm, but he didn't mention the engine or the ocean highways, possibly fearing that it might make Wankel appear dangerously eccentric.[1]

Figure 15. Gerd Steiler von Heyde-kampf, head of NSU.

NSU had been producing motorcycles and Italian-designed Fiats before the war and had reestablished itself financially after the war by producing an inexpensive moped known as the NSU Quickly. It had a 50cc two-stroke engine and was immensely popular because it was cheap, simple, and above all available. Germans emerging from the war had little to spend, but even if they had the money, often there were no manufactured products like motorbikes to be had. NSU filled the gap with their easy to produce moped and were rewarded with brisk

Figure 16. Walter Froede, NSU chief engineer.

sales that gave them the funds they needed to rebuild their business and their line of motorcycles. After becoming CEO von Heydekampf was eager to start producing automobiles again, and NSU's first re-entry into the car market was the Prinz, a small, stark, underpowered box that only a war-torn, vehicle-hungry country could love.

After going to work for NSU in 1951 to build a rotary valve motorcycle engine, Wankel continued to push his idea for a rotary engine on the company. He was told several times that NSU did not have the funds to take on such a long range project, so he tried to sell it elsewhere. He approached Dr. Ferry Porsche but was given the same answer. Because of an earlier contract that he had with Borsig, a German compressor company, he was able to convince von Heydekampf that the other company was interested in backing his engine, first as a compressor design, then as an engine, and if he didn't intervene with supporting funds, he would miss the chance to be part of the new engine. While this agreement eventually turned out to be hypothetical, it gave Wankel the leverage he needed to get Frankenberger and von Heydekampf to commit to sharing in the development costs.

Wankel then designed and built a rotary compressor. It was the first machine Wankel built that resembled the engine we know today. It used a nearly triangular (trochoidal) inner rotor moving inside an epitrochoidal outer rotor. Both moved concentrically around a stationary shaft, inside a stationary housing. Built to be used as a supercharger for motorcycles, it proved remarkably effective in boosting the power output of small engines. In one application, NSU used it on a 500cc two cylinder motorcycle and produced 110 horsepower. In 1954 they applied Wankel's compressor to their 50 cc Quickly and set a speed record of 120 mph at the Bonneville salt flats.

There was no eccentricity in the motion of the two rotors. They both revolved around the central shaft in a pure circle. The inner and outer rotors were geared to turn at different speeds; the inner rotor completing two revolutions for every three revolutions of the outer one. The difference in speed enabled the tips of the inner rotor to follow the surface of the outer rotor and produced the chamber volume changes necessary for compression. Intake and exhaust were controlled by ports in the inner rotor and the central shaft.

Geometry of the Wankel

The unique shape of Wankel's compressor and later his engine is built around the lines drawn by rolling one circle around another. If a point is chosen in or on a circle, and the same circle is rolled around the periphery of another circle, the path followed by that point is said to be a trochoidal curve. If the rolling (generating) circle travels around the outside of the stationary (base) circle, the curve generated is called an epitrochoid. If the generating circle travels around the inside of the base circle, the curve is called a trochoid. A point chosen on the periphery of the generating circle will describe an epicycloid when rolled around the outside of the base circle and a hypocycloid when rolled around the inside. All of these can be drawn with a child's toy called a spirograph, and make interesting shapes if the radii of the two circles are not even multiples of each other. When they are, the shapes become less interesting, but more useful (from an engineering standpoint).

The basic shape of the Wankel engine is described by choosing a generating circle of radius equal to one half the radius of the base circle. The point chosen to describe the line should be one half the distance from the center of the rolling circle to the periphery. The resulting shape will be the two-lobe epitrochoid, the shape of the Wankel's working chamber. Wankel worked out the shape of his engine by cutting out paper gears, one fitting inside the other, and attaching a pointer to the outer gear for a pencil to follow. As the gear ratio was two to three, rotating the outer gear around the inner traced the path of the epitrochoid that made the working housing.

A line drawn across the narrowest part of the working chamber is called the minor axis of the engine. A line drawn across the longest part is the major axis. These figures are often used to describe characteristics of certain engine designs. Other terms encountered in the study of Wankel engines are rotor apex (the point on the rotor where it contacts the housing), rotor normal (a line drawn perpendicular to the line tangent to the rotor housing where the apex meets the housing), rotor center (the point where three equidistant lines drawn from the rotor apexes to the interior of the rotor meet), eccentricity (the distance between the rotor center and the mainshaft center, and the K factor (the ratio of rotor radius over eccentricity).

By choosing a rolling circle whose radius is one third the radius of the stationary circle, the resulting epitrochoid will have three lobes instead of two. The rotor would then necessarily be a four lobed affair. By reducing the radius of the rolling circle by multiples of the stationary circle, the number of lobes in the epitrochoid will rise; a four lobe chamber using a five lobe rotor and so on.

Experiments were done by Wankel and other companies on variations using different geometries. His early experiments were done without the benefit of mathematical analysis; Wankel had arrived at the shapes he used in his machines through intuition and experimentation. Professor Othmar Baier of Stuttgart did the mathematical analysis that showed the shape to be an epitrochoid, knowledge that would streamline further analysis of engine designs. The possibility of different shapes was practically endless, but Wankel focused mainly on the characteristics of compression potential and the leaning angle of the apex seals.

The design considerations of compression ratio and seal leaning angle were determined largely by the K factor, the ratio of the radius of the rotor divided by the eccentricity of the engine. The eccentricity of the engine was

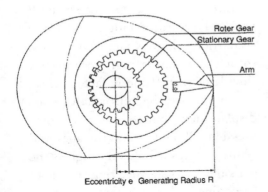

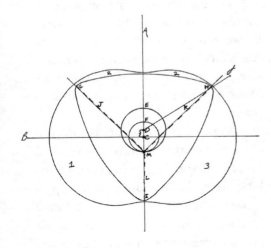

Figure 17. Wankel determined the shape of his engine by fastening a pointer to a paper disk with a gear wheel cut inside it. The gear wheel ran around a stationary gear at a 2:3 ratio. The path followed by the pointer traced out the shape for the engine.

Figure 18. If a point A is chosen on the radius B, C of the circle D, and circle D is rolled around circle E, a line will be drawn by point A describing an epitrochoidal curve. If the radius of circle C is exactly one half the radius of circle E, the result will be the two lobed shape used in the Wankel engine. The distance of point A from point C will determine the eccentricity of the engine.

Figure 19. A = minor axis; B = major axis; 1, 2, 3 = working chambers; C = mainshaft center; D = eccentric center; E & F = phasing gears; G, H, I = rotor apexes; J, K, L = rotor normals; M = point where rotor normals intersect and also intersection of phasing gears; $\mathscr{d}$ = leaning angle of apex seals, distance C–d = eccentricity of engine distance; D–H = radius of rotor

Ratio of $\dfrac{\text{rotor radius}}{\text{eccentricity}} = \dfrac{\text{distance D–H}}{\text{distance C–D}} = $ K factor

determined by the distance of the point describing the line of the shape of the working chamber from the center of the generating circle. Once the K factor is determined by the designer, the variations in compression are limited by the engine's dimensions, not like a piston engine where any engine builder can alter compression ratios by fitting different pistons. While alterations in the cavity on the face of the rotor can affect the compression ratio, once the K factor is set, the engine can be built only up to a theoretical maximum compression. For a given swept volume in engines of identi-

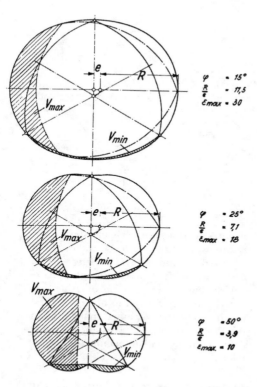

$\varphi = 15°$
$\frac{R}{e} = 11.5$
$\varepsilon_{max} = 30$

$\varphi = 25°$
$\frac{R}{e} = 7.1$
$\varepsilon_{max} = 18$

$\varphi = 50°$
$\frac{R}{e} = 3.9$
$\varepsilon_{max} = 10$

Figure 20. These drawings from a paper by Walter Froede represent three different engine designs of equal displacement, but different K factor. Where e = eccentricity, R = rotor radius, φ = seal leaning angle, and ε_{MAX} = maximum possible compression.

It can be seen that as the eccentricity goes down, the rotor and housing must be made larger. By increasing the eccentricity, the engine can be made much smaller, but as the K factor ($\frac{R}{e}$) becomes smaller the seal leaning angle φ becomes impossibly high. Most engines are designed with a K factor around 7.

(Printed with permission of the Society of Automotive Engineers, paper number 610017. Copyright 1961 Society of Automotive Engineers, Inc.)

cal rotor width, an engine can be built with a large rotor radius and small eccentricity (high K factor) or a small rotor radius and a high eccentricity (low K factor). If the K factor is low, the engine can be very small for its displacement, but its potential compression will be low and the apex seal leaning angles will be very high as the seals must cross a very tight chamber "waistline." As the K factor goes up, the engine's physical size will increase, the potential compression will increase and the maximum seal leaning angle will decrease. K factors necessary for diesel-like compression ratios tend to produce engines that are very large for a given displacement. Most practical Wankel applications have a K factor between 6 and 10 as engineers try to reach a compromise between physical size, seal leaning angles and the many other considerations that come into play.[2]

Wankel's study of rotor and housing configurations covered a range of shapes beginning with a two-lobed rotor in an ovoid housing up to a four lobed rotor in a three lobed housing. High volume automotive oil pumps often use this configuration though they don't require the sealing system that an engine would. Of the different configurations that he studied he settled on the trochoid rotor in a two-lobed housing for his compressor. Like most air pumps, Wankel's supercharger could, with some modification, be made into a four-cycle internal combustion engine by adding a compression and expansion cycle to the already existing intake and exhaust.

Eventually, NSU gave Wankel the go-ahead to convert his compressor into a four cycle engine. He was invited to do his work in NSU development shops, but he preferred to work on his own turf; indeed, Wankel had a reputation of being a difficult colleague so it was probably better that his work was mostly done in his private institute as Lindau. He had working with him an old friend, Ernest Hoeppner, who had a reputation as a brilliant designer who was able to convert abstract ideas into practical designs. It took them over three years of work to convert the compressor into a running engine, and their product was hardly the model of elegance and simplicity that we later came to know as the Wankel rotary. It was in fact at least as complicated as any reciprocating engine ever was. Like the compressor, there were an inner and outer rotor spinning together, the inner turning twice for every three revolutions of the outer. The air intake remained in the stationary center shaft, but the ports were gone from the rotor faces. Air intake was directed through the inside of the inner rotor, out ports in its sides, and through channels in the outer rotor. Intake was controlled by the relative position of the inner and outer rotors. The exhaust port was set in the outer perimeter of the outer rotor. Because combustion took place between two rotating parts, there was no fixed location for the spark plugs. They were installed inside the inner rotor with the tips facing outwards. To fire the sparkplugs, slip-ring type connections had to be installed inside the inner rotor. Simply changing the sparkplugs with this configuration would mean removing the rotor completely from the engine in order to access its interior.

The first engine was labeled the DKM54, or *drehkolbenmoter* (rotary piston engine) 54, indicating the displacement in cubic centimeters. It first sputtered to life in a test stand in February of 1957. Had the Wankel remained in that complex form, it never would have raised an eyebrow in the automotive industry. But as such, it was simply a test mule, built to test theory behind the trochoidal chambers and the methods and materials of proposed sealing systems.

There were indeed many complicated shapes to seal. The sides of the rotor were challenging because the shapes of the seals were gently curved lines, not straight lines or circles. The corners were also an interesting problem requiring many moving elements, but it was the apex seals, the seals at the tips of the inner rotor separating one rotor face from another, that bore the larger part of the combustion load. Each element of the sealing issue would give Wankel ample opportunity to test the sealing systems which he had patented and had spent so many years developing.

In most past and current versions of Wankel's engine, the side seals are single strips of metal set into a groove running alongside the length of the rotor face. The strip is spring loaded by a wavy metal piece of spring steel set underneath it. It is the task of this seal to maintain combustion sealing on one side, and control oil leakage on the other side, much like a piston ring in a reciprocating engine. But the motion of the strip is far different from a piston ring as the seal strip sweeps across the flat surface in an arc instead of moving only in a direction perpendicular to its length. Though the movement is complex, and the shape unusual, acceptable side sealing has been achieved using systems no more complex than this. Most experiments done in side seals involve different materials and strip widths.

At each rotor tip, the apex seals and the corner seals come together in effort to isolate each rotor face from the others. At any given time, the three rotor faces are engaged in different portions of the engine's working cycles. It is the job of the apex seals to keep these processes separated from each other. The apex seals are strips of a sealing material which ride in grooves cut into the rotor tips. They are lightly spring loaded, only to assist in sealing during start-up. When the engine is running, the centrifugal force on the seals is enough to keep them pressed against the surface of the inner rotor. Later, drillings and passages would be added to the apex seals in a variety of configurations by engineers of all the different companies that worked with the Wankel for the purpose of introducing gas pressure on the back side of the seal to supplement the spring force. The corner seals consist of movable pins that are spring loaded in the ends of the rotor tips, bearing against the side plate of the outer rotor. Grooves are cut into the pins to accommodate the ends of the outer sealing strips. The corner seals are rather complex, because they must form a union where the ends of the apex seals and the side-seals meet. The years to come would see many variations on the corner seals, but the essential theme would remain the same. Based on Wankel's earlier patent for sealing around an irregular opening, the side-seals and apex seals would end in a movable, spring loaded pin whose sides are grooved to allow all the elements of the seal to move independently.

All of the seals would present problems as they were developed over the years, but it would be the apex seals that would prove the most confounding. Harder seal materials lasted longer, but caused rapid wear of the rotor housing. NSU preferred to use softer material in favor of not wearing out the working surface of the housing, beginning with certain carbon compounds. They hoped that through their design they could make the engine so easily serviceable that changing the apex seals would be a minor operation taking only a few hours. The search for the proper material would be like Thomas Edison's search for the proper material for his light bulb filament. The list of substances that would not work would grow very long before truly acceptable materials would be found.

A few months after the DKM54 took its first breaths, a larger version was built, the DKM125. Again, it was a test mule, sharing many of the problems of the 54 and acquiring a few of its own associated with its larger size. As Wankel had predicted, the engine ran at very high speeds, much higher than a piston engine. Volumetric efficiency, a measure of how much air an engine pumps compared to its displacement, was found to be 98 percent at 7000 revolutions per minute. At 16000 rpm, it had only fallen off to 70 percent, still a very good figure for a gasoline engine. All this meant that the Wankel

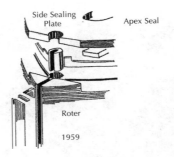

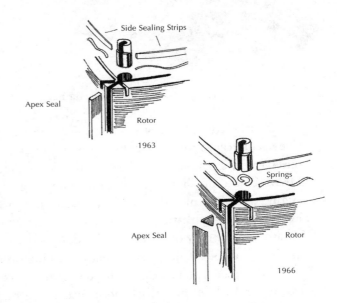

Figure 21. Sealing systems. Over the years, all the companies working with the Wankel would try out many different sealing grids. Top left is Wankel's original version which used a movable plate for the side seal and a five piece apex seal. The most successful systems were the simplest, as in the 1963 version used by NSU, where the apex seal was a single piece. Later engines employed extra pieces at the end of the apex seal to accommodate variations in rotor size due to temperature change.

would be most effective running at much higher speeds than a conventional piston type engine, which is usually limited to about 6000 rpm. In fact, after constructing a special safety tunnel to protect the lab and its occupants from exploding bits, the engine was tested at 25,000 rpm without failure. But the high rotational speed and the large mass of the outer rotor produced a very high rotational inertia, so the engine, once running at one speed, was reluctant

Figure 22. The DKM125 engine.

to change speed, not a suitable characteristic for an automotive engine. Another effect of the running speed was that it exerted tremendous centrifugal force on the outer rotor, causing small but significant distortions in its shape, and eventually degrading the effectiveness of the seals.

Neither the DKM54 nor the DKM125 was at all practical for automotive use. Because the center shaft was stationary, the power was drawn off the outer rotor. This would make transmission coupling very complicated. The DKM125 did not have a proper outer housing; the stationary portion of the engine was the center shaft and the outermost part was essentially a case having no contact with the working parts of the engine. If the Wankel were to go any farther, it would have to be designed with installation and practical use in mind. But Froede was already working on that.

Froede had picked up on an idea that Wankel had studied and rejected earlier, and while the DKM motor was being built Froede began work on a modified version. He converted the outer rotor to a stationary housing and made the central mainshaft a moving piece which would be the output shaft. The mainshaft gained an eccentric lobe for the inner (now the only) rotor to turn on, and the rotor would now orbit the center of the mainshaft as well as turning about its own center. Froede's name for the modification was a kinematic inversion. It's a difficult motion to visualize. The rotor would swing about the center of the mainshaft like a hula hoop, pushing the eccentric shaft ahead of it, The shaft would be rotated one complete revolution for every third of a revolution of the rotor. Since the rotor had three working faces, this produced one power stroke per revolution of the output shaft, the equivalent of a two-cylinder four-cycle piston engine.

Ironically, it was the introduction of this complex motion that gave the Wankel its simplicity. Now that the outer rotor was gone, intake and exhaust could take place through ports placed in the housing. The sparkplugs could

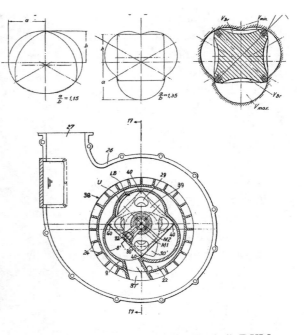

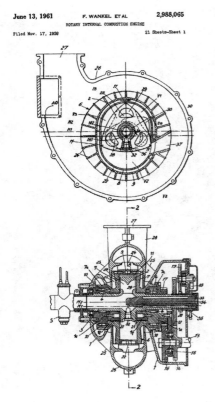

Figure 23, *left.* **Patent drawings for Wankel's DKM engine. The center shaft is stationary; the inner rotor spins freely on the shaft but is geared to the outer rotor. Power is drawn off the outer rotor and the external housing collects the exhaust from the engine spinning inside. Figure 24,** *right.* **Wankel's experiments were not limited to the three sided rotor. These patent drawings show that his thinking went beyond to a four sided rotor in a three lobed chamber. Other notes showed studies of a five sided rotor in a four lobed chamber.**

now be accessed through the outer housing instead of through the center of the rotor, and their location could easily be changed in the course of development work. Cooling systems were simplified. The engine could now be mounted in a vehicle, rather than just a test stand, and a conventional transmission could be attached.

The new engine was dubbed the KKM125, KKM being an abbreviation for *kreiskolbenmotor*, or circuitous piston engine. Froede and his staff built two versions, one with an iron housing which weighed 37.4 pounds and one with an aluminum housing weighing 23.2. It was the fusion of all the pieces, the epitrochoidal chambers, Wankel's sealing systems, and Froede's eccentric motion, that produced the first practical Wankel rotary engine.[3]

Initially, Wankel was very unhappy with Froede's modifications. He had rejected the kinematic inversion in principle during his earlier studies as being a bastardized rotary engine because of the combination of the eccentric motion. Wankel's fixation was pure circular motion and he did not want to be concerned with anything less. He railed against Froede's engineering staff saying that these young people always think they know better and had made a cart horse out of his race horse. He called his DKM engine the true connecting link between the piston engine and the turbine and protested the violation of his original design.[4] Among other arguments, he expressed concern for the life of the apex seals, as the eccentric motion introduced them to new stresses. His concerns about the apex seals were valid, as it was the eccentric component of the new engine's motion that introduced

Figure 25. Felix Wankel with the DKM125 prototype of 1957.

the steeper leaning angles of the seals relative to the outer housing. That and the inertial forces brought on by traveling around the eccentric shaft did indeed make the apex seals' difficult job even harder. But Froede was eventually able to convince Wankel of the practicality inherent in the new design. NSU was not having a good year, and Froede's research department had been nearly shut down several times for lack of funds. Von Heydekampf pulled enough weight with the board to keep the program alive, but he could not afford to fund development of both versions, so he stopped all work on the DKM in favor of the KKM because it seemed to hold the greatest promise for immediate practicality.

The issue of displacement would arise time and again with people trying to evaluate and classify the Wankel. Wankel himself even devoted an entire SAE technical paper to the subject of calculating the displacement of his engines. While it may seem inconsequential, it became important as the engine came into more and more popular use not only because engineers needed a benchmark for comparison purposes but also because governments must tax anything that moves and they like to measure things before they tax them. Later displacement would become important for racing officials as they

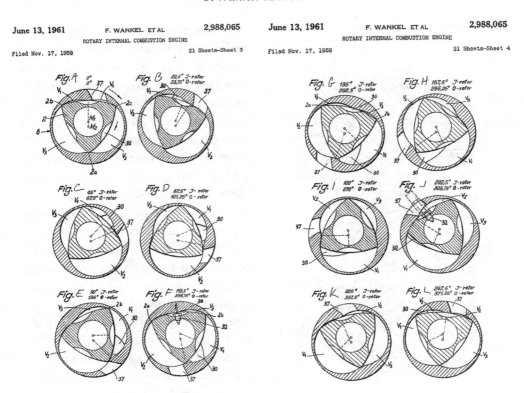

Figure 26 A–L. A portion of Wankel's patent on the DKM. To explain the motion of the DKM requires no fewer than 12 drawings. The outer rotor is the driven member and turns three times for every two turns of the inner rotor. In figures A and B, V_1 is beginning its intake cycle as the intake port (30) opens up. The exhaust port (37) passes the rotor tip and moves on into V_2. The intake cycle for V_1 continues until figure J wher ethe intake port passes the rotor face for V_1 and is closed off. Compression begins for V_1 in figure K and continues in L. The continued process can be seen by picking through the compression and combustion cycles.

tried to decide where to allow the Wankel-engined cars to compete. People who came to own Wankel-powered cars, particularly the racers, preferred to express the displacement in terms of the maximum volume of one individual working chamber multiplied by the number of rotors. By this formula the engines seemed outrageously small for their power output, and it would fall into the smaller tax bracket or smaller racing class. But more careful analysis showed that this was the equivalent of lumping four cycle engines with two cycle engines. Because a single cylinder engine produces one power stroke per revolution of the output shaft and a single rotor Wankel produces two, most sanctioning bodies and governments agreed to multiply the maximum chamber volume by two and multiply that figure by the number of rotors.

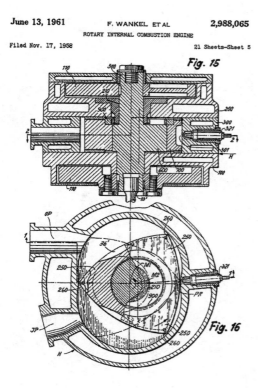

June 13, 1961   F. WANKEL ET AL   2,988,065
ROTARY INTERNAL COMBUSTION ENGINE
Filed Nov. 17, 1958   21 Sheets-Sheet 5

Figure 27. Patent drawing for the KKM engine, the basic design of the Wankel engine that we know today.

The eccentric motion introduced by Froede did come with its own set of problems. The new engine was not as completely vibration-free as the original rotary, and all sorts of new stresses were introduced. But the simplification brought on by the new design was easily worth the burden. The Wankel was now something that could be made useful after some development.

Among the problems found with the new design was turbulence of oil inside the rotor. The rotor was oil cooled, and therefore full of oil at all times. The combination of the eccentric and spinning motion of the rotor churned up the oil in the rotor until its inertia began to soak up power. The power robbing effect is similar to what can be felt when trying to walk across a room while carrying a container filled with a sloshing liquid. The motion of the liquid tends to maintain its own velocity and moving it in another direction can require a lot of force. The violence of the motion of oil inside the rotor was fully appreciated when engineers tore down an engine that had suffered an untimely rotor failure. A small metallic fragment had been accidentally left in the rotor when the engine was assembled. The motion of the oil inside the rotor was sufficient to pound the fragment against the inside of the rotor until it had worn completely through. NSU experimented with fin shapes for the inside of the rotor and were able to produce a device to better control the flow of oil through the rotor while the engine was running.

Froede and his staff were also troubled with repeated bearing seizures. They tried needle bearings on the eccentric shaft, but would later determine that it was not a bearing problem at all, but distortion of the rotor itself that led to seizure. By changing the rotor material from light alloy to cast iron, they were able to stop the bearing problems. So in the interest of simplification, once they had settled on cast iron as a material for the rotor, they returned to the use of plain bearings.

Cooling also became an issue with Froede's version. Since the outer rotor was now a stationary housing, combustion always occurred on one side of it, and intake on the other, giving rise to a hot side and a cold side. This seemed a pretty easy problem to solve; simply rearranging the cooling passages would transport more coolant over the hot side. But the area around the sparkplug presented a special problem. The casting to accommodate the sparkplug openings interrupted the flow of coolant past the hot side of the housing, causing local overheating severe enough to result in cracks in the housing around the sparkplug. Continued work on cooling system design eventually brought this under control to some extent, though it would continue to be a problem for every company trying to develop a Wankel of its own.

A well-developed version of the KKM125 developed 26 horsepower at 11,000 rpm, a respectable output for an engine that only weighed 37.5 pounds. For further research, Froede built a larger version, the KKM250. The 250 was designed for studying certain details of power production such as combustion chamber shape and optimizing the location of the sparkplug. By mid–1959, the KKM250 was undergoing testing.

In order to study the combustion characteristics in the Wankel, particularly flame front propagation, Froede built a special housing, one that had multiple sparkplug fittings at five points along the outer perimeter. A sparkplug was placed in one fitting, and ionization detectors in the others. In this way, it was possible to measure the effect of the sparkplug location on the movement of the flame front. What the engineers found was surprising. The gas that was squeezed out into the larger part of the working chamber by the rotor face as it approached the minor axis moved faster than the flame front could spread. The situation could be improved with sparkplug location and changes in the fuel mixture, but a large amount of unburned gas was invariably left over after the combustion cycle. This unresolved problem would haunt everyone who tried to develop the Wankel for street use during the 1970s because the unburned gas would end up in the exhaust manifesting itself as unburned hydrocarbons (HC). But in 1959, nobody was worried about exhaust content except for what it could tell them about engine operation.

Experiments were also done with multiple sparkplug installations. It was found that using two plugs didn't accelerate combustion at higher engine speed, but two sparkplugs placed along the perimeter of the housing and firing sequentially did improve low speed performance and idling. Also, sparkplugs could be placed each in the ideal position for low or high speed operation and fired under different conditions.

As the problems with the KKM250 were ironed out, NSU began to look

Figure 28. The KKM250 as first installed in an NSU Prinz.

at building a Wankel driven automobile. Company stockholders were nervous and there were rumors questioning the feasibility of this new engine they had invested in. A prototype automobile would be just the thing to quiet things down. In 1960, the 250 was installed in a standard NSU Prinz, a basic subcompact car already in production, and several journalists and people from the automotive world were invited to drive it. It was crude and difficult to drive, and the engine installation was clearly a hurried and undeveloped project, but it did drive, and it proved that the Wankel could be adapted to automotive use. Some even generously allowed that even in its crude and undeveloped state, it was an improvement over the conventional two cylinder engine that normally came in a Prinz. NSU still had a long way to go to achieve any kind of reliability, however. More prototypes were built, and as they cruised the roads of Europe racking up test miles they would succumb to new and challenging problems. An unmarked truck affectionately known as the "Hearse" would pick up the stranded cars and return them to Neckarsulm for more study.

Later the KKM400 was built, simply a larger version of the KKM250. It could produce 40 to 50 horsepower, more than enough to drive a small car with ease. The prototype engine was fitted up to a conventional Volkswagen transaxle and installed in a similar production car, the NSU Sport Prinz (a fastback version of the standard Prinz sedan). Development had paid off: The Sport Prinz was easier to drive than the first prototype Prinz, smoother and more powerful, in spite of the fact that most components of the drivetrain were selected more for their ease of installation than their suitability.

The motoring press was kinder this time. "When I put my foot down on the throttle and engaged the clutch, I realized very quickly that I had something special in hand. From 2000 to 6000 rpm the engine might have been a gas turbine, so smoothly did it run. ... The performance was almost too good for what was obviously a pretty experimental combination of engine, gearing and automobile. The KKM400 Prinz did every thing very well without incident or complaint, so that I did not have the feeling of pioneering a new invention. It was more like driving a new sporting version of some engine and a commendably quiet one at that."[5]

The KKM400 and other early Wankels were lubricated by a pressure system as well as by adding oil to the fuel, like a two stroke. At that time, emissions were not a concern, and the need to lubricate the rotor tips required the additional oil. They tended to consume oil from the sump as well. The oil was pumped into the rotor for cooling and bearing lubrication and would leak to some extent past the side seals to be burned in the combustion chamber. Early Wankel proponents remarked that the engine would never need an oil change; it would just consume a predictable amount and the owner would just add to the oil at regular intervals. Others were less easily convinced and predicted that the engine could never be made suitable for automobiles because of its oil consumption.

The Sport Prinz prototype was a tremendous boost to the credibility of the NSU-Wankel engine. The original Prinz was not the stuff to impress automotive journalists. Normally it was powered by a two cylinder, air-cooled engine of 26 horsepower and weighed in at 1200 pounds. At 50 horsepower, the KKM400 engine brought a lot of life to the dry little car in spite of the hastily installed Volkswagen gearbox whose standard ratios were poorly matched to the engine. Its performance went a long way to convince skeptics that the new engine cooked up by NSU might have a real future in the automotive industry.

4

Curtiss-Wright

Curtiss-Wright Corporation is an American company that is a direct descendant of the company founded by the Wright brothers for the purpose of building and marketing their flying machines commercially. In the twenties, the Wright company merged with a company founded by Glen Curtiss, who sold the U.S. military its first airplanes. The new company was involved in all phases of aircraft and engine manufacturing for the first half of the century. After World War II it became primarily a defense contractor supplying aircraft, but mostly aircraft engines. In 1949 Roy Hurley became president of the company. Known as an autocratic leader, Hurley was strong in his opinions. But Max Bentele, an engineer who worked for Hurley, knew him as the ultimate expediter. If you were working on a project that Hurley wanted, you got everything you needed almost before you needed it.

Bentele was a German born and schooled engineer who had spent the war years working on turbine blade design for Germany's new jet aircraft, the Heinkel-Hirth HE078. After the war he found work managing a machine shop that also belonged to Heinkel-Hirth. It had been left standing, and some of the former employees were working, making household items for people in the surrounding town, but the management was gone. Bentele stepped into the vacuum. Some French officers of the occupying force once approached him with a box of broken parts from their American built Jeeps and asked him if he could manufacture them. There was apparently some animosity between them and the American forces, which Bentele found privately amusing, and they hoped to be able to keep their vehicles running without depending on the Americans for spare parts. From those parts, he put together a spare parts manufacturing and supply business that lasted long after his departure.

He left the machine shop at the request of the Americans and the British who wanted him to come back to the aircraft shop to help them repair and study the scuttled and damaged jet aircraft left behind by the Germans. He put together a team that built a dozen new aircraft for the Allies to study and continued his studies of turbine blade design. While he was there he was interrogated by various Allied officials, many of whom were also engineers, and during these interviews he made his contacts that would eventually lead him to immigrate to America to work for Curtiss-Wright, but not right away. He stayed in Germany with the Heinkel-Hirth company long enough to establish a thriving moped business based on a motorcycle not much different from NSU's Quickly. From there Bentele accepted an offer from the British Ministry of Supply to work on a turbine engine for a ground car. It was during this project and his connection with Bosch, L'Orange and Daimler-Benz for fuel injection equipment that he again met the men from Curtiss-Wright who were able to persuade him to come to the United States.

Curtiss-Wright had been manufacturing some of the best aircraft and engines in the world for decades but was caught asleep at the switch when the turbojet engine began to dominate the aircraft industry. For years its biggest engine, the TC18, had been supporting the company in military and civilian applications. It had been through many evolutionary changes, with turbochargers added on top of turbochargers in order to extract every possible bit of horsepower, but it was becoming dated as the industry was turning toward turbojet and turboprop engines. Bentele was given the task of looking for yet more ways to improve it. Some of his modifications were adopted enthusiastically, while others were met with stonewall resistance. In this way Max Bentele was introduced to the politics of American corporations.

Curtiss-Wright was working on a new jet for the military and had one turbojet in production, but Bentele was not allowed to see them because he lacked the security clearance to work on them. From what he had seen of the civilian versions, he suspected that Curtiss-Wright was far behind in jet technology. The technology was moving very quickly and the Curtiss-Wright jets were fast becoming obsolete. Eventually, the government contracts they had hoped would be their redeeming stroke were awarded to Pratt and Whitney and General Electric, Curtiss-Wright's biggest competition, so the financial plug was pulled on the new turbojet.

Hurley responded by trying to extend the life of the existing company products and diversifying into other types of transportation. He tried to sell the TC18 to the railroads as the ultimate powerplant for a prop-driven high-speed train. Though the concept was not unprecedented—Germany had a prop-driven passenger train during the 1930s called the Schienen-Zepplin—the railroads were unimpressed with the idea. He proposed converting the TC18 to run on diesel or jet fuel to make it more versatile, but that proved too complicated an undertaking and the project was abandoned to the thankful sighs of many Curtiss-Wright engineers. Tests were done with mufflers in an attempt to make the TC18 as quiet as a jet, but the results of that were also disappointing.

Other adventures looked good at first, but failed to make a lasting impression. The company built a personal hovercraft and demonstrated it at Rockefeller Center. It caused quite a stir as it rose off the ground, the cushion of air blowing up the skirts of the ladies in attendance, but that project was also abandoned because of difficulties in development of roadholding and braking characteristics.

Hurley had acquired control of Studebaker Packard, which was working on a fuel injection system for its cars, and it was a visit to Germany by one of their representatives that led to his being introduced to the Wankel. During a meeting between William Hannaway of Studebaker and representatives of Kugelfischer, a manufacturer of carburetors and fuel injection systems, Hannaway learned from the Kugelfischer representatives of the new engine that NSU was working on, so he visited NSU to learn more about it. At that time (1958), NSU was not yet highly protective of its technology, and Hannaway was given a model of an engine to take back home for his company to study.

Hannaway gave the model to Hurley, and Hurley gave the model to Max Bentele and asked him to take it home over the weekend and study it. He asked him to come back on Monday and report whether it was worth pursuing. In his autobiography, *Engine Revolutions*, Bentele remembers the incident.

> Full of anticipation, I showed the new and exciting contraption to my wife. She remarked, "Judging from its geometry, it looks elegant. If it works it could be great." Studying the "engine" in detail step by step, I discovered that the arrangement represents an ingenious combination of the efficient four stroke principle, the simple two stroke valving mechanism, and a near rotary motion. The engine offered low bulk and weight with additional advantages over reciprocating engines: more uniform torque, less vibration, and less sensitivity to fuel octane number. Whether all these advantages could be

achieved in practice would depend on satisfactory solutions to its problem areas: gas and oil sealing, cooling, ignition and combustion. On the whole I arrived at a positive conclusion.[1]

On Monday morning, he reported being impressed with the engine, but very conservative about its potential, having seen for himself the potential problems of developing it, particularly the problems of sealing the rotor tips. When he learned from Hurley who had designed the engine, he expressed his confidence in Wankel, having been familiar with his work on sealing systems during the war.

Shortly after that meeting with Hurley, Bentele and Hannaway flew to Germany to meet with officials at NSU. Hannaway was just about to introduce Bentele to von Heydekampf when von Heydekampf interrupted and said, "Don't bother. We know Bentele very well. In the scooter years he was our fiercest competitor."[2]

Bentele advised Hurley to be conservative and try to negotiate an option to buy a license rather than a full license until the engine's potential could be further evaluated. Hurley offered NSU $50,000 for such an option, but NSU apparently thought they were being made a pathetically low offer for a license and von Heydekampf rejected the offer, saying, "We don't take tips."

NSU's early attempts to patent the engine in the United States did not go smoothly and were nearly scuttled because the attorney they hired did not know his U.S. patent law well. They were mounting an appeal when Curtiss-Wright discovered their difficulties and used them as leverage to negotiate a license agreement. Bentele and Hannaway told von Heydekampf that it was only because of their earlier gentlemen's agreement that they were bothering to negotiate a license at all. They pointed out the botched patents and argued that they could produce rotary engines in the United States without a license if they so chose, according to Bentele, von Heydekampf eventually conceded that NSU had no patent protection in the United States. Bentele and Hannaway agreed to use Curtiss-Wright's resources and influence to help them straighten out their basic patents.[3] NSU's version of the story was that the patent application was eventually straightened out by the diligent efforts of Dr. Froede and Wankel. Either way, on October 21, 1958, Curtiss-Wright became the first company to purchase a license to produce Wankel engines for $2.1 million and a 5 percent commission on all Wankel engines that Curtiss-Wright would build and sell. The agreement also stipulated that technical developments and patents would be shared by the two companies as they both continued to work on the engine. Curtiss-Wright would hold exclusive rights to the Wankel in the United States and could sell licenses to other

American companies, but it had to have NSU's permission to sell to a company that produced automobiles or motorcycles. The license was good until 1964, at which point they could still collect royalties for engines produced by other licensees.

While with NSU, Wankel himself had taken a very active role in financing the development of his engine. He had formed a company, Wankel GmbH, with Ernst Hutzenlaub, a German inventor and a shrewd businessman, and Peter Lindenmayer, a German engineer who had spent some time with Curtiss-Wright. The purpose of the company was to sell licensing agreements to other companies to produce Wankel engines. Hutzenlaub insisted that Wankel GmbH receive 50 percent of all income from any future licenses. NSU balked initially, wanting to give Wankel only 24 percent. The board was reluctant to give more because German law gave a 25 percent shareholder rights to block certain board actions that have a significant effect on company structure. Reluctantly, however, von Heydekampf bumped his offer to 35 percent and the parties eventually settled on 40 percent with the stipulation that Wankel would take on a 40 percent share of the research and development.

Once a license had been acquired by Curtiss-Wright, Hurley asked Bentele if he would head up the R&D program on the new engine. Bentele accepted, selecting for his staff Charles Jones and Ferdinand Sollinger, and began working out plans for the development program.

They decided that the engine needed more thorough analysis than NSU had been using in order to fully understand its problems. NSU, they felt, was working too empirically, working like mechanics instead of engineers and trying to solve their problems with trial and error rather than engineering theory. So they began with a full mathematical analysis of the stresses and loads in the engine from which point they intended to design out the problems. But Hurley was in too much of a hurry for that. When Bentele told him that they might be eight years developing an engine suitable for an automobile, Hurley was furious and nearly fired him then and there. He then began throwing company resources at the Wankel, removing engineers from their regular positions and assigning them to the Wankel project. He frequently showed up in the lab to provide help and supervision, solicited or otherwise.

The general public knew little about the Wankel rotary, but there were sufficient rumors of "the engine that would make everything else obsolete" to excite investors. Nevertheless, Curtiss-Wright worked on the engine as though it were top secret. But when they invited some engineers from the Perfect Circle Company in to help them with seal design, one engineer, seeing the sketches that Bentele made, exclaimed, "That's a Wankel engine!" He had seen one at Volvo in Sweden. The Curtiss-Wright people were shocked. They had thought that no one outside of their own skunkworks knew anything about the engine. So Hurley decided to go public. On November 23, 1959, Roy Hurley took out full-page advertisements in several major papers. He released a film of a small engine pumping water for fire hoses, and made bold sweeping projections about the new engine's possible uses. Curtiss-Wright stock quickly rose by about 50 percent. Talk of the "engine of the future" went over well with speculators until the announcement came later that the company would be cutting dividends because of poor profits. Investors began to feel like they'd been had and Hurley found himself in front of the Securities and Exchange Commission convincing them that the Wankel was for real, not a scheme for manipulating company stock, and that he intended to develop it to its full potential.

Things were getting crazy on the other side of the ocean as well. Speculators began buying up NSU stock at ever increasing prices. For years the majority of NSU stock had been held by the Dresdner Bank. It had been doing poorly for a long time and the directors decided that, now that it was profitable, it was time to unload the troublesome company. Hurley was interested in purchasing the stock and gaining controlling interest in the company that received his license fees, but Hutzenlaub and von Heydekampf intervened and convinced the bankers that they should not be party to an American takeover of the historically German company. The bank then began selling its stock in small amounts to an eager public on the open market.

NSU took advantage of the trend and issued new stock in 1960, but the general public was not invited. This drove market prices even higher and NSU stock peaked on June 30, 1960, at 3200 percent of par value. (European investment firms listed stocks in percentages of par value. The average German industrial stock might trade at about 300 to 400 percent of par.) Taking advantage of the trend, the Dresdner bank sold the last of its holdings in NSU. The speculators took the hint and began selling off their stock at ever falling prices.

Von Heydekampf was naturally concerned about overinflated stock prices, and investors were very suspicious and touchy. Each new rumor would send stock prices soaring, and Von Heydekampf would have to issue a qualifying statement, reiterating that their rotary engine research was strictly a long term investment, to calm things down. At one occasion, a shareholder wrote to NSU and asked when it might be possible for him to buy a vehicle with a Wankel engine. Without von Heydekampf's permission, his letter was answered by his assistant, Dr. Hirsch. Dr. Hirsch replied that NSU would be starting production of a 400cc engine of 45 to 55 horsepower and offering it in an automobile and a boat the next year. The market again rose rapidly, and Dr. Hirsch was asked to leave the company.

Hurley's early enthusiasm for the new engine and his aggressive marketing strategies continued to cause trouble for him over and above his difficulties with the SEC. NSU and Wankel in particular were angry about his press release that almost neglected to mention them at all and implied that the rotary engine was a brilliant new product of Curtiss-Wright. Hutzenlaub flew to New York, booked a conference room at the Waldorf–Astoria and told Hurley that if he did not go public and admit that the engine was a German invention, he would give a press conference and explain the truth. Hurley conceded and later issued a statement explaining the engine's origin.

Roy Hurley's interest in new technologies may almost seem visionary in retrospect. In 1960 he got the company involved in solar energy, fiberglass propellers, and his proposed vertical takeoff and landing airplanes using swinging propellers. But his vision did nothing for Curtiss-Wright's short-term profits. His bold manner and aggressive tactics continued to lose friends for him at the company as well as overseas, and he was attacked at the company's annual meeting in a series of critical speeches. In 1960 he resigned as head of the company and was replaced by a more fiscally conservative three-member executive committee headed by T. Roland Berner.

Berner and his committee initially were suspicious of the Wankel program, thinking that the engine was an elaborate scam devised by NSU with the possible involvement of Max Bentele. Berner returned from a visit to NSU a believer but assured the board that there would not be any engines produced nor any details publicized until there had been considerably more development on the engine and all ideas and designs were proven sound.

So the board decided to go on with developing the Wankel. Bentele and Charles Jones were kept in their positions to continue the work they had begun under Hurley, but Bentele was relieved of many of his administrative duties associated with the project. He enjoyed this demotion as it allowed him more time to work with the engine rather than shuffle paper.

With, or perhaps in spite of, Hurley's help, Bentele and Jones learned enough in six months to build an improved version of their own. After thoroughly studying all known aspects of Wankel design, they'd settled on a design of 60 cubic inches, using many of the geometric proportions from Wankel's first engine the DKM54. Their prototype was labeled the IRC6. In its first dyno test, in 1959, the IRC6 developed 100 horsepower at 5500 rpm.

Bentele and Jones felt that the NSU cooling system would be inadequate for a high output engine. The NSU system fed the coolant into the housing and circulated it around the periphery to the outlet. Because combustion takes place on one side of the engine and intake on the other, the engine had problems with unequal heat loading leading to stresses and eventual distortion of the castings. Bentele and Jones designed a cooling system that circulated axially, along the length of the engine, then returning to the front. They built their end housings from iron and laid out the cooling jackets on their engine such that the coolant traveled past the high heat areas quickly, through tighter passages, and moved more slowly, even doubling back, in low heat areas. The cooling passages were streamlined and laid out with no abrupt changes in direction to cause stagnant areas which would lead to hot spots and steam pockets in the end housings. They designed a rotor housing with a thin wall and reinforcing ribs that ran at an angle from one end housing to the other. The ribs formed passages linking the cooling passages of the two end housings. NSU and Curtiss-Wright had been experiencing the formation of "chatter marks" on the inside of the rotor housing. The marks were lines or ripples across the surface of the housing that sometimes even broke through the chrome surface of the housing. Bentele felt that they were a result of high speed bouncing of the apex seals on the reinforced parts of the rotor housings. By running the reinforcing ribs at an angle, there would be no inconsistency in the elasticity of the rotor housing surface, so theoretically, the seals would ride on the surface in a more uniform fashion.

At first Bentele and Jones liked the light alloy rotor for their engine, for its heat conductivity as well as its light weight. The rotor was oil cooled (also like NSU) from the inside with passages guiding the oil beneath the hot working surfaces. Initially it seemed to work well, but under hard endurance testing, there was a problem with the apex seals wearing the edges of the seal slot as they were forced first against one side, then the other by combustion pressures. For a time Bentele and Jones considered using hardened inserts in the apexes of the rotor where the seal grooves were, but instead they built a rotor out of cast iron.

Ironically, where NSU had experienced rotor distortion with alloy rotors, Curtiss-Wright had distortion problems with its iron rotor. Tests with the iron rotor looked good under low load, but as the load increased, the power output of the engine became erratic and unpredictable. Engineering analysis showed that small thermal distortions were affecting the fit of the rotor in the housing under some operating conditions. The internal ribbing had to be redesigned several times before the problem was considered to be solved with a rotor having an internal I-beam type of structure.

Test results with the I-beam rotor were encouraging enough that the

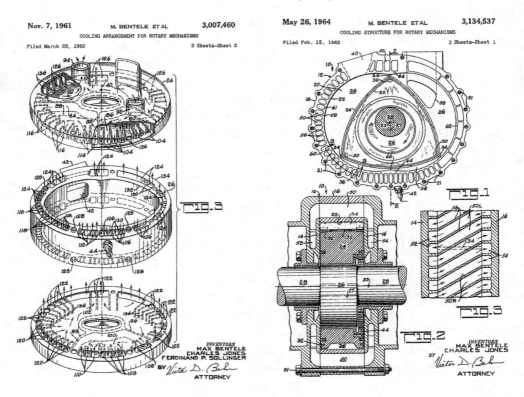

Figure 29. Patent drawings for Curtiss-Wright's cooling system. The coolant was directed across the rotor housing from front to rear, rather than around it as in the NSU engine. The ribs inside the trochoid housing were angled to distribute the load of the apex seals running along the inside.

engineers pushed for higher rotational speeds and higher power. The next part to break down was the molybdenum surface of the rotor housing and, consequently, the apex seals. Different materials were needed for the rotor housing surface. Cast iron housings with a nitrided surface were tried next. Nitriding is a metal hardening treatment familiar to builders of automotive racing engines. The nitrided surface was easier on the apex seals, but the nitriding process itself caused small distortions in the housing's surface and reduced the seal's effectiveness under heavy conditions. The engineers later tried applying molybdenum to the housing surface with a spray which could be ground true after application. After good tests with iron housings for a time, they gave the same treatment to a housing made from aluminum and had satisfactory results. Eventually, this process would give way to chrome plating of the aluminum housing interior which worked well with a cast iron apex seal.

Unlike NSU, Curtiss-Wright chose to locate the intake ports in the end housings instead of the periphery of the rotor housing. It was clear that by admitting the charge through a side port, there was less mixing of exhaust with the fresh charge and the intake could be closed earlier. It was analogous to camshaft timing in a conventional engine. A Wankel engine with intake ports in the side covers behaved like a piston engine with a "milder" camshaft because the nature of the intake cycle could be better controlled. There was more torque available at low speeds, and the engine was more tractable, while a peripheral port engine had higher total output, and behaved a little poorly at idle and low operational speeds, like a conventional engine with a high performance camshaft.

Running the Wankel engine with conventional automotive ignition systems worked only for a little while. As the power output went up, so did the heat and pressure, and the conventional sparkplugs couldn't take it. So special sparkplugs with unusually cold heat ranges were developed, but this resulted in frequent fouling. Changes were made to the plug end design to reduce fouling, but the problem couldn't really be called solved until a special capacitive discharge ignition system was designed that increased spark voltage from fifteen to sixty thousand volts. This change extended sparkplug life in the Wankel by a factor of ten.[4] The capacitive discharge ignition was so successful in extending sparkplug life and maintaining reliable fire under harsh conditions that versions of it would later show up in the automotive aftermarket as high performance equipment.

After extensive testing and redesign, the IRC6 engine had evolved into the RCI-60. Still a single-rotor engine, still displacing 60 cubic inches and having the same geometric configurations as the IRC6, it sported all the benefits of the last three years of development. A special engine was built to explore the high speed potential of the design. This engine had a peripheral port housing and produced 154 horsepower at 7000 rpm. Torque was over 120 foot-lbs. from 4000 to 6000 rpm.

In 1963, Charles Jones began work on a twin rotor version of the RCI-60 for possible automotive applications. It was designated the RC2-60 U5. By September of that year the first one was running happily on a test bench. The engine performed fairly well under a variety of endurance tests, but to some extent, many of the original problems with the engine remained. Seal tip wear, chatter marks on the housing, and difficult cold starting were still present. Jones was not discouraged, being convinced that the engineering was good, but he had to refine and develop the cooling system in order to maintain control of thermal distortions of seals and other critical engine components.

Figure 30. The RC260 engine as configured for automotive application.

He was not concerned about leakage around the side seals, as it was minimal and any gas that did leak past the sides of the rotor was vented into the intake ports. Leakage past the trailing apex seal was not a large problem either because the gases that did leak ended up in the next chamber to be burned again on the next ignition. But leakage on the leading apex seal was a matter of great concern and the center of development activity for a long time to come.

Jones found consistent patterns in housing wear that were reducing the effective life of the apex seals. Without a completely true and flat surface to ride on, the seals could only deteriorate more and more quickly as they wore to conform to the changing surface of the housing. So to solve the seal problem, he concentrated on the housings. Under dyno testing, chrome plated housings were wearing at a rate of .001 inches for 200 hours of operation. By 1965, a new material had been developed, a very expensive alloy whose composition was kept secret for a while. Using this new coating, housing wear was virtually eliminated. A 528 hour test, 30 percent of which was run at wide open throttle between 3600 and 5000 rpm, showed only .0000421 inches of wear.[5]

In 1965 the RC260 engine reached a point in its development where it was showing comparable durability to piston type automobile engines. New developments of the rotor oil seals had reduced leakage past the rotor to the point that it was necessary to

Figure 31. Components of the RC2-60.

Figure 32. William Figart inspects the installation of an RC2-60 engine in a 1965 Ford Mustang.

design in a certain amount of leakage to keep the rotor sides lubricated. A certain amount of oil was also fed to the apex seal slots to lubricate the apex seals as they ran along the trochoidal track of the rotor housing. Oil consumption had been reduced to levels that were acceptable for piston engines of the time. The next step was installation of the engine in an automobile for real-world testing.

A 1966 Ford Mustang was the first test mule for the RC260 U5 engine. The original engine in the Mustang was a 200 horsepower 289 cubic inch V8 coupled to a three-speed Ford Cruise-O-Matic automatic transmission. The equivalent displacement of the Curtiss-Wright engine was 240 cubic inches and the rated output was 185 horsepower at 5000 rpm.

Much of the Ford equipment was retained in the swap. The automatic transmission was kept in spite of the fact that its shift points were not designed to take good advantage of the new engine's torque characteristics. The alternator and ignition system from the Ford were also adapted to fit the new engine, and a two barrel carburetor was fitted from a Buick.

Jan Norbye, then automotive editor for *Popular Science* magazine, was given the opportunity to test drive the Mustang for an extended period. For his article, Curtiss-Wright would not allow him to reveal what kind of car was being used for the test. Perhaps they were concerned about starting rumors that Ford was planning a Wankel-engined Mustang. Ford had shown little or no interest in the Wankel and rumors of that kind could have been very awkward for both companies.

Like other automotive writers before and after, Norbye first remarked about the sound of the Wankel, a strangely quiet but powerful sound, and an eagerness to rev.

> It had a steady idle at 800 rpm and a dab on the throttle sent the revs up to 2000 in a flash. Above 2000 rpm it began to develop a new sound—a sound I had never heard before. I have driven gas turbine cars. I remember the scream of the supercharged BRM 16 cylinder racing car; and I have been in Ferrari's test house with four V-12's going at full bore. But this was a new sound.
>
> As the engine began to wind, the pitch was lower than a turbine's, although there was something of a turbine in it. Yet it had the evenly pulsating rhythm of a good six in perfect tune—without giving any indication of reaching top speed when pushed to the 6000 mark. It would seemingly go on and on accelerating forever."[6]

In automotive trim, Curtiss-Wright claimed oil consumption of one quart in 1100 miles of driving. They claimed also that they had solved the sealing problems and their engine could go for 100,000 miles or more between overhauls. Different versions were built and tested for marine applications. An RC260 U5 was put in a 2½ ton Reo truck for testing by the military, and an air-cooled version was developed for possible use in aircraft. Many of the different sizes and applications were under parallel development before and during the time that Jones was working on the automotive engine, so by the time Jones's project reached fruition in the Mustang, Curtiss-Wright had a large family of Wankel engines for a variety of uses.

Max Bentele had seen early on the possible benefits of stacking up several engine units in modular fashion and had applied for patents on a four-rotor design as early as November of 1959, only a few months after the first successful test of the single-rotor IRC6. While stacking up two chambers is a fairly straightforward affair, there are complications that arise when trying to build an engine with more than two rotors. In a two rotor engine, it is not necessary to support the eccentric shaft with a center bearing. But as the shaft gets longer to accommodate more rotors, it must be supported by bearings at

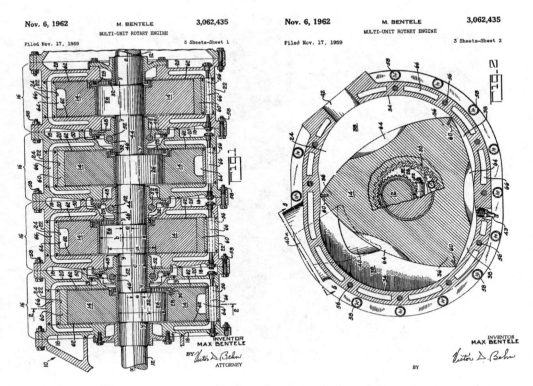

Figure 33. Patent drawings of Curtiss-Wright's four rotor Wankel designed by Max Bentele.

each segment. Since the bearings and timing gears cannot be passed over the eccentric portion of the shaft during assembly, they either must be split or the eccentric shaft must be built up in pieces. Bentele decided against piecing the shaft and designed an integral bearing-gear assembly that was split along the axis considered to have the lowest bearing load. The engine was assembled by first fitting the eccentric shaft into the front housing. The gear and bearing assembly was fitted, then the rotor and rotor housing placed over it. The end housing was placed over that, then the next bearing-gear assembly was installed and bolted to the former end housing. The end housing for the next chamber was fitted which had a wide enough center hole to fit over the gear, and the next rotor and housing were installed, and so on...

The four rotor engine was designated the 4RC-6. The first multi-rotor Wankel engine ever built, it produced 425 horsepower at 6500 rpm. It was later to lead to the building of a four rotor, air-cooled aircraft engine designated the RC4-60 J2. The engine used many of the design features developed during the research on the RCI-60. But work on the engine was

Figure 34. RC2-60 installed in a 2½ ton army truck.

discontinued early because the military market that Curtiss-Wright had hoped
for to sell the engine never developed.

As part of their development program for the Wankel, Curtiss-Wright
held extensive research on the engine's possible multi-fuel capability. Bentele
decided early in the program that the Wankel's design did not lend itself to
the high compression ratios required for compression ignition. Higher compression ratios could be easily achieved by altering the K factor (the ratio of
rotor radius to eccentricity), but that took the engine design out of the para-
meters where he considered it to be reliable. So he concentrated instead on
several layouts using high pressure injection and spark ignition.

Bentele designed and patented several versions of the RCI-60 engine for
heavier fuels in the diesel and JP aircraft fuel range. The engine used a direct
fuel injection like a diesel, but the fuel spray was injected across the electrodes
of a spark plug. Some arrangements used a pre-chamber, like a diesel, and
others sprayed the fuel across the plug, directly into the rotor housing. Of the
different layouts tried, the most promising consisted of an injector fixed such
that the spray pointed towards the oncoming face of the rotor, placed about

Figure 35. The Curtiss-Wright test cell in the 1960s.

10 degrees after the minor axis. Using spark ignition, Curtiss-Wright engineers were able to run this engine on JP4, JP5, #2 diesel and high octane gasoline. The power output was necessarily lower, because of the lower pressures of the slower, controlled burn but the advantages included lower exhaust temperatures, smaller cooling system requirements, lower hydrocarbon and carbon monoxide emissions, and the obvious versatility of an engine that could run on practically any fuel.[7] The engines of this type became known as the DISC engines, for direct injected stratified charge.

The experimenting was not limited to any specific size either. At one time Bentele and his staff built an RC-6 engine times 30, literally 30 times larger in its basic dimensions, giving it a displacement of 1920 cubic inches. Its test output was 872 horsepower at 1525 rpm. At the other end of the scale, they built a 4.3 cubic inch air-cooled motor that produced 3.5 horsepower at 4000 rpm. The large engine didn't produce power proportional to its size because the speed of the flame front couldn't keep up with the charge moving through such a large engine. The small engine was simply too expensive to be practical in its potential applications.

By 1966 Curtiss-Wright had designed, developed and tested Wankel engines from one extreme to the other. They were the first to build a multi-rotor

Figure 36. Wankels in all sizes from Curtiss-Wright. *Top left*, RC1 air-cooled 4.3 cubic inch lawnmower engine. *Top right*, portable generator powered by RC2-60. *Bottom left*, RC2-90 air-cooled aircraft engine. *Bottom right*, SCRC4-350 four rotor, stratified charge engine displacing 350 cubic inches.

engine, and they had built the largest and the smallest Wankels yet. But most importantly, they had developed the RCI-60 and its twin brother, the RC2-60, to the point that they were practical automotive and marine engines. They had proven multi-fuel capability for military applications and were working in the aircraft applications. Curtiss-Wright was ready for their first big Wankel contract, but other companies in other parts of the world were catching up fast.

In 1967 Max Bentele decided that his work on the rotary was done as far as Curtiss-Wright was concerned, and he left the company for a position with AVCO Lycoming. Rotary engineering was left in the capable hands of Charles Jones, and Jones continued working on the engine while the management waited quietly for their first big rotary contract. It was a contract that unfortunately would never materialize. Other companies bought patent licenses, producing some revenue from the Wankel, but nothing like the millions spent over the last ten years of development. In the opinion of Bentele and other industry observers, the management of Curtiss-Wright was too conservative about marketing the Wankel. Had the company looked more actively for that big contract, they suggested, it might have materialized.

In 1984 Curtiss-Wright would sell its rotary business, technology and license to Deere and Co., more commonly known as John Deere. The $14 million deal represented a substantial loss for Curtiss-Wright. Deere, having acquired a bargain in technology, hoped to succeed in marketing where Curtiss-Wright had failed. Throughout the 1980s Deere would pursue markets in heavy equipment, aircraft and military equipment applications.

5

Toyo Kogyo

Toyo Kogyo, better known especially outside Japan as Mazda, was once a small engineering firm based in Hiroshima, Japan. The name means "Oriental Cork," which has as much in common with their products of today as the Skinner's Union or "SU" name seems to have with the famous carburetors that they produced. Nevertheless, the company founded by Tsuneji Matsuda in 1920 did begin by producing cork products. Later, it shifted to building bicycles, and progressed to building some motorized models. The company dabbled in motorcycles for a time, but had little success with motor vehicles until beginning production of three wheeled delivery trucks in the 1930s. The trucks, which had more in common with a motorcycle than a car, looking more than anything like a Harley Davidson servicar, became more and more popular in the years leading up to the war. They were called Mazdas, for the Matsuda family's name. By 1940 Toyo Kogyo was selling up to 1500 of these "trucks" a year and was planning its first four wheeled car when its facilities were shifted over to producing weapons for the Japanese military.

Toyo Kogyo had an enviable location for a Hiroshima company, not far from the city, but separated from it by a small range of mountains. This fortunate location saved the company from destruction while most of the city was wiped out by the atomic bomb blast in 1945. Some glass was broken and roofs were damaged, but the buildings themselves were spared, as were their occupants. Matsuda once remarked that only the employees that were absent from work were killed that day. After the war was over the company rebuilt as much as possible. By 1947 Toyo Kogyo had restarted its prewar production line of small trucks and resumed its efforts to get into automobile production.[1]

Kenichi Yamamoto was a young mechanical engineer who had graduated in 1944 from Imperial University in Tokyo. He loved aircraft and hoped to go into a career in aircraft design, but with his country at war, there was little employment other than war production available. So, staying in his field, he found himself designing landing gear for fighter planes. By war's end, he had been commissioned in the Japanese Navy and was working on a Japanese fighter called the Wild Orange Blossom, the infamous Kamakazi fighter plane that was not designed to land at all, but to explode on impact.

The conclusion of the war found him among the unemployed in a part of the country where most of the industry had been trashed. He was more fortunate than most in that that his home had been spared, and he was able to go to work at the area's only surviving factory, Toyo Kogyo.

Yamamoto was a talented engineer, but he had to take what work he could find in his devastated country. He went to work on the assembly line building transmissions for three wheeled Mazda trucks. He made a living, but found the work repetitious and boring. To add a little interest to the work, he found some plans on his supervisor's desk and with his permission, studied the drawings, checking them against the gearboxes he was building. Eventually his ability and attention to detail were noticed by someone in the design department and he was offered the opportunity of a job in engine design.

Yamamoto was assigned to design a new and more powerful overhead valve engine to replace the anemic little side-valve unit in the Mazda trucks. He began the project by visiting motorcycle shops. Before the war the British motorcycle industry had the lead in small-engine technology and produced some of the best examples of overhead valve designs to be found in small, air-cooled engines. British bikes were rare in postwar Japan, however, and what privately owned bikes were in the country were mostly black market purchases that were kept hidden from curious strangers. But Yamamoto was able to slip into the right circles and convince people with examples of Triumphs, Nortons, and Sunbeams hidden under tarps in dark corners of their shops to let him have a look.

He was taken by the design of a Triumph vertical twin, finding the cylinder head to be his idea of a model of elegance and simplicity. He lifted much of the cylinder head design from the twin and applied it to his own design, a 60 degree vee twin of 1157 cc. The engine went into production in Mazda's new type CT truck and was an instant success in a vehicle-hungry Japan.[2]

Toyo Kogyo continued to improve and enlarge its vehicles throughout the 1950s, but the management was looking for an edge. Particularly, they wanted something to establish a unique identity for the company to save them from being nationalized or eventually taken over by the larger Japanese auto companies of Toyota and Nissan. Wankel's rotary engine was breaking news in 1959 and Matsuda, the company president, realized that it could possibly be just what he was looking for. The engineers for Toyo Kogyo began to study the news of the engine as it came filtering out of Germany and also studied analysis and opinions from the automotive community around the world. By the time they attended the Wankel Symposium which was sponsored by the Verein Deutscher Ingenieure (sort of a German SAE) in January of 1960, their opinion was that the Wankel did indeed have a future in the automotive world and that Toyo Kogyo should be a part of it.

In many ways, Toyo Kogyo was a natural for the job of developing the Wankel. In the Matsuda family, the company had leadership that was interested in taking risks on emerging technology, and they had a good track record for embracing new manufacturing methods. They were the first company outside the United States to build a computerized production line. Earlier, in the 1950s, they had brought into Japan methods and technology for sand casting small and complex shapes, like the Wankel's trochoid housings and rotors. They also made many of their own machine tools, which gave them an advantage when learning to produce the new and unusual shapes found in the new engine.[3]

But getting a piece of the Wankel turned out to be a lot harder than anyone expected. The engine was causing quite a stir and little Toyo Kogyo had to get in line behind about 100 other companies wanting to sign up to produce it. It was only through the intervention of Dr. Wilhelm Haas, the West German ambassador to Japan whom Matsuda had befriended in the spring of 1960, that they were able to get a foot in the door at NSU. In October of 1960, President Matsuda and five of his technical staff went to Germany to work on an agreement. They were shown tests and data on the KKM125, 250 and 400 and were shown Prinz automobiles undergoing field testing with KKM250 and 400 engines. NSU engineers impressed the visiting Japanese with the engine's balance and lack of vibration by balancing a coin on its side on an engine while running at high speed in a test stand. On October 12 the agreement was signed, later to be approved by the Japanese government in July of 1961.

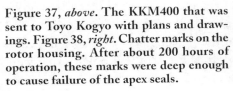

Figure 37, *above*. The KKM400 that was sent to Toyo Kogyo with plans and drawings. Figure 38, *right*. Chatter marks on the rotor housing. After about 200 hours of operation, these marks were deep enough to cause failure of the apex seals.

In 1960 anyone daring enough to buy into an NSU patent received for their trouble a KKM400 prototype engine, some blueprints and prospects of much development. Toyo Kogyo engineers dismantled, studied, and reassembled the NSU engine, then built a prototype of their own. It behaved in much the same way that NSU's early engines did: it shook, it smoked, and it drank oil in large amounts. After 200 hours in the test stand, it failed. A post-mortem found what were commonly described as "chatter marks" on the housing surface. Much as in the Curtiss-Wright testing, they were small, repeating gouges across the surface that eventually had led to separation of the surface plating and destruction of the seals. In that state, the engine didn't seem at all like something that could take on the established auto industry. But Tsuneji Matsuda, the son of the company's founder and now president of the company, liked the idea of the rotary, and he still felt that it could give his company that special technological edge if it could be made to work. He called Kenichi Yamamoto to his office and assigned him to select a staff and form an independent department to research and develop the Wankel rotary engine.

Yamamoto was excited by the opportunity of groundbreaking engineering, but apprehensive about the outcome. The responsibility was huge and the budget was a large burden on the relatively small company. But the payoff could be big, a completely new powerplant to make their automobiles unique in the market, possessing performance characteristics that could be found nowhere else. To make a commitment to the development of an infant technology was not a decision that would likely have been made in the boardroom of an automotive giant. The automotive industry is far too conservative for that sort of thing. The decision to finance the project could only be made by a person in the unique position of Matsuda—an owner-operator, as it were. Yamamoto saw Matsuda as a man of great vision and was determined not to let him down. He was given the use of an old building with a few test stands to begin work with the promise of a new facility to be constructed for research and development in the immediate future.

Yamamoto held the opinion that, for all its faults, the rotary engine was not inherently flawed, but rather the metallurgy and machining technology of the time were not up to the rotary's advanced design. He assembled a small team of metallurgists, designers and engineers to tackle the identifiable problems that were known to exist—problems of seal tip wear, chatter marks and wear on the running surface, breakage of the phasing gears, oil consumption, and erratic, unstable low speed operation. In short, all the problems that were all too familiar to NSU. Toyo Kogyo approached these problems by relentlessly experimenting with new materials and techniques for using them, hoping to hit on the right combination. By the time Yamamoto and his team had gone from the first prototype in 1961 to their first production model, the 110S, they had amassed a pile of nearly 5,000 junk rotary engines in the back lot behind the workshop.

In 1964, Toyo Kogyo completed a new, state of the art test laboratory to replace the dark old building that had been housing Yamamoto's rotary division. There were basic test cells and endurance test cells linked by centralized controls capable of running endurance tests 24 hours a day. Data from the test cells, 30 in all, was handled by computer for easy reference and interpretation. The ready availability of the numerous test stands and the automation that made it unnecessary to man the cells continuously streamlined testing for the development of a product that would have to undergo an enormous amount of testing.

Yamamoto's engines were designed with light-alloy rotors, iron end covers and aluminum trochoidal housings. The surface of the housings was electroplated with chromium. This produced a hard, smooth surface for the seals to ride on. The seals were fairly soft, made of a carbon-aluminum composite. In an early attempt to solve the problem with chatter marks, a series of holes were drilled across the base of the seals, and another hole drilled along the length. Yamamoto's team felt that the marks were a result of the seals vibrating at their own resonant frequency during operation and hoped that the drillings would reduce the high-frequency vibrations of the seal that they thought were causing the damage.[4]

The drilling helped reduce the chattering of the seals, but it wasn't considered a very practical solution for use on production model engines. While it did demonstrate the soundness of the engineers' theory as to the origin of the marks, such precision drilling was time consuming and delicate, therefore expensive, and it made the seals more fragile. So work on different seal materials and configurations continued.

Early experiments with seal materials included imbedding carbon with a variety of different metals, aluminum becoming the metal of choice. The aluminum flakes gave the soft carbon seals more strength while maintaining the self-lubricating quality of the soft carbon. Toyo Kogyo used this material until the early seventies, when engineers would decide that the stiffness of a cast iron seal would do the job better.

Later developments in the rotor housing involved a new process called transplant coating. Essentially, it was a process intended to reduce the time that the trochoidal housings had to spend in the chromium plating tank and thereby speed up production. The chromium plating did not adhere well to aluminum, but it did adhere to steel; and steel would adhere well to aluminum. So the casting die for the housing was first sprayed on the inner trochoidal core with steel. Then the molten aluminum was poured into the die after it was pre-heated. What came out was a steel coated, die-cast aluminum housing that could then be machined and plated with a very thin layer of chrome. The process improved the adhesion of the chrome plating to the housing because of the intermediate steel layer, and saved money in production because the housings didn't have to spend as much time in the plating tank.

Early prototype engines also tended to break their phasing gears. The engines would be running in the test stand and then begin to behave as though they were having some kind of epileptic fit, said one engineer. When the engines were torn down, it was found that the phasing gears were broken to pieces. After developing a method to measure electrically the stress on the teeth of the gears, Toyo Kogyo engineers modified the shape of the teeth until breakage was no longer a problem.

Another problem Toyo Kogyo experienced that had been seen at NSU was the formation of cracks in the rotor housing around the sparkplug holes. It was determined that they were a result of "thermal shock" or the sudden thermal loads placed on the housing when it was taken from a relatively cool temperature and sharply accelerated to 7000 rpm in all the gears on a road test. By developing a test bed procedure that could consistently reproduce these conditions, engineers could then do systematic studies on cooling system improvements and their effect at relieving thermal loads. Tests were showing that on cars driven hard immediately after startup, the temperature of the inner wall of the rotor housing reached 450 degrees F within one minute of startup. This abuse consistently produced cracks in the housing around the sparkplug openings after 4,000 cycles.

Improvements in the cooling system brought the maximum temperatures of the rotor housing trochoidal wall to below 410 degrees F. But the final improvement was the redesign of the housing itself. The bosses for the tension bolts which held the engine together were relieved from the inner wall of the housing, thereby relieving part of the mechanical restrictions on the part that gets the hottest. Repeated testing after this improvement produced no more cracks in the housings.[5]

Mazda mixed oil with the fuel for rotor tip lubrication like NSU, but instead of pouring it in at the tank, they did it mechanically. A small metering pump linked to the accelerator was designed to control the amount being injected. In the early models, the oil was injected into the fuel bowl of the carburetor; later models would have the oil injected directly into the rotor housings.

Like Curtiss-Wright, Yamamoto and his staff preferred the benefits of intake ports mounted in the end housings rather than those mounted in the periphery of the rotor housing. They had performed similar experiments in this area and agreed that there was a reduction of high speed power production, but felt that the greatly enhanced tractability of the engine was well worth the trade. The engineers would change their minds about this issue several times before finally settling on side ports (i.e., ports on the housing ends) for their production engines.

Yamamoto and company could afford to trade off some high speed performance for tractability because they were concentrating on building a two rotor engine instead of a single. They had made this decision very early in the development process, even before they had developed a suitable single rotor engine. Their intention was to develop a powerplant that was adequate to drive a medium sized car, an engine of 100 horsepower or more.

To further improve low speed driveability characteristics, Mazda added another ignition system. Like NSU, Mazda found that the optimum spark plug location was different for low and high engine speeds. The plugs were placed in their respective optimum locations, and fired five degrees apart, the lower plug being the first (leading) plug and the one mounted higher in the housing being the trailing.

The additional sparkplug had another advantage of helping to control engine knock due to pre-ignition. At low speeds, lighting the sparkplugs five degrees apart kept detonation to a minimum. This turned out to be helpful for the selection of different apex seal materials as the softer seals were very quickly destroyed when detonation occurred.

While the leading sparkplug was located in a hole the same size as its end, the same was not true of the trailing plug. At the point where the rotor tip passes the trailing plug, the difference in gas pressures on either side of the apex seal is huge. If the hole were as large as the sparkplug, when the rotor tip passed the hole, combustion pressure could leak into the adjacent chamber. To prevent gas leakage, the sparkplug was recessed away from the internal surface of the housing and connected by a small transfer port through which the fuel mixture could pass and be lit by the plug.

Mazda was not shy about demonstrating its commitment to the Wankel rotary even before it had a fully developed basic unit. While Mazda engineers were still working on the KKM400 they built prototypes of three and four rotor engines, and had a prototype of their first production rotary car, the Cosmo, ready for display at the 1963 Tokyo Motor Show. Though it wouldn't appear in the show until 1966 and would not be mass produced until 1967, its appearance beat NSU for the introduction of the first twin rotor Wankel production car.[6] Toyo Kogyo had originally planned to show the Cosmo at the Frankfurt Motor Show in 1963, but NSU was also planning to put a rotary car in that show and not wanting to be upstaged, they "reminded" Mazda that their license deal at the time only permitted them to sell their cars in Asian countries. The Japanese relented and as far as the world was concerned, with the Spider, NSU introduced the world's first car built for rotary power.

The Mazda Cosmo, Japan's first car built especially for the rotary engine.

The Cosmo was a two-seat sports car designed specifically for the rotary. The first engine to power the Cosmo had a design radius of 105 millimeters and an eccentricity of 15 millimeters, giving it an R/E ratio of 7:1. It had a single chamber displacement of 491cc. Using the displacement formula of twice the chamber volume times the number of rotors, it was regarded as a 1964cc or roughly a two liter engine. It had cast aluminum rotor housings, chrome plated on the running surface. The rotor housings were sandwiched between three cast iron end housings that were induction hardened with a radial stripe pattern on the working surface. The process produced a good, hard surface for the rotors to run against without warping the housings as would happen if the entire housing were hardened.

Initially, the Cosmo engine had peripheral intake ports in the rotor housings, but later, Mazda went to side ports to improve the torque at low speeds. The peak torque was brought down to a lower speed, enhancing the car's driveability, but peak power was seriously affected.

Another engine was built for the Cosmo, slightly larger, to regain the performance lost in the changeover to side ports. This engine had dual sided intake ports, the ports in the center housing being connected to the primaries of a two stage carburetor, and the outer ports connected to the secondaries.

The Cosmo went into very limited production in 1967. Eighty cars were built and lent to some of Mazda's key suppliers and dealers for field-testing. For the duration of testing, the cars performed well and reliably for 80,000 miles or more, but the top speed of 98 miles per hour seemed slow for a lightweight two-liter sports car. Mazda engineers then added a peripheral intake port to be run off of the secondary barrels, keeping the side ports for use at low speeds and small throttle openings. This improvement brought the power curve up and increased the top speed to about 115 miles per hour. Mazda continued to produce the Cosmo, with a variety of engine configurations, but never in large quantity. In five years, only 1176 were made.

At this time, Mazda had plans for two other rotary powered cars. The RX 85 was to share a body with a conventional car, the Mazda 1000. It would later become known as the R 100, a car that was well received in Japan and later in the United States in spite of its extraordinarily high price of $2500. Mazda was cautious at first in America, starting with dealerships in Washington state, then Florida, then Texas. The Florida market flopped, mostly because people in Florida weren't buying any type of import car in 1969, let alone one with a strange new engine. But the West Coast sales were picking up fast, fast enough that dealers began lining up for the opportunity to buy a Mazda franchise.[7] The Cosmo was interesting, but it was expensive and in

Figure 40. The Mazda R100, the first rotary-powered car imported to the United States in quantity.

short supply. But the R100 sedan was getting some good press and people were interested to see what would be coming next.

What came next for Japan was the RX 87. First appearing at the 1968 Tokyo auto show, it was renamed the R130 and was sold only to Japan's domestic market. Fitted with a larger version of the 8020 engine linked to a front-wheel-drive transaxle, it represented the high end of Mazda's rotary automobiles.

Mazda introduced the RX-2 in 1970. It was a rotary version of the car called the Capella, which was also available with a piston engine as the Luce

Figure 41. Mazda's R130 was a front wheel drive luxury coupe sold only in Japan.

Figure 42. The RX-2, known in Japan as the Capella.

in Japan and the 616 in the United States. The RX-2 was Mazda's first rotary to be sold in large numbers as America counts them.

The early talk about how inexpensive it would be to produce Wankel engines proved untrue for Mazda, or any of the other producers for that matter. While it was true that the engine had far fewer moving parts than a piston engine, the moving parts that it did have were complex and expensive to make. The rotors and their housings were shaped unlike anything else in the automotive industry, and there was little automated machinery available for the job, so Mazda was forced to machine many of the engine's parts using slow, manually controlled machinery. The first, and for a long time the only, automated machine for grinding rotor housings was a German machine known as the Kopp grinder, which could grind housing surfaces at the rate of six per hour. It had no competition until 1970 when a Swedish inventor named Nils Hogland built a cam-guided trochoid grinding machine, the Tru-Choid, that he claimed could grind 24 trochoid housings per hour. By then, other machine tool manufacturers were getting into the act and building their own versions of trochoid grinders. The machines were expensive, to be sure, but were essential equipment for any company even considering large scale Wankel work.[8]

Toyo Kogyo had spent over $50 million in the 1960s bringing the rotary to the point of development it had achieved. The product, they felt, was sound enough for the market and they had placed all of their hopes for their independence on the success of the rotary. Fortunately, the company's conventional products had continued to sell well enough to keep them solvent, but only just. By 1970 Toyo Kogyo was running on the ragged edge financially, and anything less than total success with the rotary cars would virtually insure that the company would be taken over by Toyota or Nissan. Realizing this, they looked to the largest automotive market in the world, the United States, to generate the sales they needed to stay afloat.

6

Work Continues at NSU

At NSU in 1963, the Wankel was beginning to get some real respect. Engineers and automotive enthusiasts had been talking about the new engine for a few years, but now articles were again showing up in business news as well as engineering journals. NSU had been shaking the bugs out of the engine in automobiles since the initial prototypes and now announced that it was beginning production of a new car, a Wankel powered Spider. Initial estimates were that the first year of production, 1964, would see 3,000 to 4,000 cars. The Wankel engine was becoming an economic reality instead of a laboratory curiosity, and businessmen were once again speculating that it could be the start of something big.

The world's first look at the Spider prototype was at the Frankfurt automobile show in October of 1963. The car was well received, but there was much skepticism that it would ever become a production car.[1] NSU was a very small company to be taking on such a project, and many industry analysts doubted that it was financially capable of developing and producing a car that was such a departure from the industry norm.

The Spider was an open, two-seat, rear engined car weighing about 1500 pounds, which was a little heavy for a car of its size. The engine was certainly lightweight, but the front-mounted radiator, coolant filled plumbing and grossly oversized muffler, which was necessary to quiet the exhaust without producing enough back pressure to affect performance, added much weight.

It is one of those engineering ironies that a lot of heavy equipment was required to make use of an engine whose most redeeming quality was its light weight, but that would always be the case until the engine was much further developed.

Apart from its engine, the NSU Spider was a fairly unremarkable car, little more than a convertible version of the Sport Prinz body. It did not handle particularly well, and the brakes were not outstanding; in short, it was just another pint-sized convertible roadster. But it did have a very special quality in its unique engine, and members of the motoring press were thrilled to drive it. One journalist remarked on how easy it was to over-rev the engine.

> I dabbed the throttle and the needle whipped around to 6000 at the end of the red "danger" zone and bounced quivering off the pin. The exhaust note rose in a swift glissando to a muffled purr. With my foot lifted, the exhaust note instantly returned to a hushed pattering.
>
> "This'll be fun," I thought. A German technician leaned over the cockpit. "Don't worry about the 6000 revs," he said referring to the redline on the tachometer, "Do whatever you want."[2]

The power curve was reminiscent of a two-stroke engine. Much of this could be attributed to the intake ports being located in the periphery of the housing. Experiments had already shown that locating the ports in the sides, or end covers, of the engine gave it more low speed flexibility, but high-speed chamber filling was more efficient with the peripheral ports. For such a small engine, this was a good choice, because it enabled more power production simply by increasing engine speed.

The engine had little to offer below 2500 rpm but would pick up quickly once above 3000 rpm, making the Spider a fun car for people who liked to shift gears. Power built well until the revs reached 7000, then began to drop off. But even so, the engine gave no sign of failure at that speed and seemed as though it could easily endure much more.

NSU was still using soft carbon apex seals in a chrome-plated housing for the Spider engine. Although engineers estimated the useful life of the seals to be about 50,000 miles, they considered this preferable to harder seals that would last longer, but were more likely to damage the chrome-plated surface of the housing. They dealt with the short seal life by designing the engine such that an end cover could be easily removed and new seals slid into place in a relatively small amount of time. Oil consumption was high by modern standards, about 700 miles to the quart, as there was a large amount of leakage past the rotor side-seals into the working chambers. But NSU recommended not changing the oil, only adding to it as necessary.

Figure 43. The NSU Spider, introduced in 1964.

Only 152 Spiders were actually produced during the latter part of 1964, but by the first quarter of 1965 there were about 600 Spiders on the road. Production numbers never reached the original estimates, but NSU was building and selling Wankel powered cars, and that fact really relieved stockholders and made the rest of the world take notice. NSU was not a large company, standing in sixth place in Germany for production numbers, and it was a very bold move for them to spring this new motor on the world. NSU had already built production Wankels for a stationary water pump, and even a self-powered water ski tow device, but such things were easy enough for the industrial world to ignore. An automobile was serious business, and deserved watching. NSU felt that they were being conservative by putting their first production Wankel in a sports car. "Sports car owners are crazy," one NSU official was quoted as saying. " They are the ones who will buy a car with a revolutionary motor."[3] It is interesting that NSU did not have a program to build a rotary motorcycle, but they were trying to become a larger car company, and a Wankel motorcycle was not in their plans at the time.

The early problems with the Wankel rotary were by now well known in the automotive community, particularly among the Big Three American auto makers. Seal tip wear, chatter marks on the housings, bearing failures, oil consumption and side gear failures had been the stuff of technical journal articles and various dissertations since the Wankel was introduced to the world in 1958. American executives still viewed the Wankel with cautious skepticism. But it was clear that the news from Nekarsulm couldn't be ignored. Publicly they dismissed the Wankel as being too "smokey"; privately they wanted to know more. With all the other potential advantages, if NSU really had solved the sealing problems, it could be a very important engine. Supposedly, at least one Spider was bought from a private citizen in Germany to be transported back to the United States for study by one of the American companies, a rumor that delighted the officials at NSU because, if true, it at least meant that the Americans were taking them seriously.

The engineers at NSU were optimistic that they had things well under control. Engines had been successfully tested in the lab for up to 1500 hours, equal to 90,000 miles. Prototypes and production cars had been driven for thousands of miles by engineers. Things were going well and board chairman, Gerd Stieler von Heydekampf, was not shy about building his entire future strategy around the new engine. In early 1965 he announced that NSU was planning a new, larger prestige type car built around a two rotor engine to be produced possibly in the coming model year

But it was the sale of rotary licenses that really kept the small company going. As NSU tirelessly developed their engine, more and more people became convinced that it might be more than just a passing fad. If you were in the car business, it could be that you could not afford to ignore the Wankel. Curtiss-Wright's initial investment of $2.1 million was only the beginning. Toyo Kogyo had come in early and was reporting progress with their Wankel. Citroën was planning a joint venture with NSU, and other companies holding licenses by 1965 were Fichtel and Sachs, Alfa Romeo, Krupp, Daimler-Benz, Rolls-Royce, and an East German government company. Russia was rumored to be experimenting without the benefit of a license.

Von Heydekampf, the director of NSU, had been approached by car makers of all sizes to make a deal for permission to produce Wankel engines. He had been in talks with both Ford and Volkswagen without reaching a deal. BMW even tried to negotiate a license by threatening to destroy NSU's patents in the courts. Von Heydekampf called their bluff and won. He was not at all intimidated by the large companies, in spite of the fact that they were large enough to swallow all of NSU whole. "They apparently thought it was too expensive," he said of Volkswagen. "Of course, they can buy it anytime they want, but it will be more expensive."[4]

With cars in the hands of customers and on the road now, mileage was beginning to accumulate. When the Spider was introduced, NSU had predicted that owners would be able to drive for about 50,000 miles between engine overhauls. By today's standards, this would seem like a short life, but in 1965, that placed it just below average for its small car brethren. The car was selling, NSU was investing in equipment to speed up rotary engine production, and major motor companies were putting up increasingly large sums of cash for the privilege of adding a Wankel rotary engine to their line. By 1966, the list of rotary license holders looked like this:

- 10-21-58, Curtiss-Wright Corporation, USA, for all applications, power output and sizes

- 12-29-60, Fichtel & Sachs AG, Germany, for small gasoline engines of .5–12 HP

- 2-25-61, Yanmar Diesel Co. Ltd., Japan, gasoline engines from 1 to 100 HP and diesel engines from 1 to 300 HP for all applications except motorcycles, automobiles and aircraft

- 2-27-61, Toyo Kogyo Co., Ltd., Japan, gasoline engines of 1–200 HP

- 8-8-61, F. Perkins Ltd., England, gasoline and diesel engines up to 250 HP

- 10-4-61, Klockner-Humbolt-Deutz, Germany, diesel engines for all applications without restriction

- 10-26-61, Daimler-Benz AG, Germany, gasoline engines of 50 HP and up

- 10-30-61, MAN Nurnberg, Germany, diesel engines for all applications without restriction

- 11-2-61, Friedrich Krupp, Germany, diesel engines for all applications without restriction

- 12-19-63, Rhienstahl-Hanomag AG, Germany, gasoline engines of 40–200 HP

- 3-12-64, Daimler-Benz AG, Germany, diesel engines for all applications without restriction

- 4-15-64, Alfa Romeo, Italy, gasoline engines of 50–300 HP

- 2-17-65, Rolls-Royce Ltd. England, diesel and multi-fuel engines of 100–850 HP

- 2-18-65, Vereinig. Volkseigener Betriebe, Automobilbau, East Germany, gasoline engines of .5–25 HP and 50–150 HP

- 3-2-65, Dr. Ing. h.c. F. Porsche K.G., Germany, gasoline engines of 50–1000 HP[5]

Considering that only been 10 years had elapsed since the first prototype engine had run in the lab at NSU, considerable progress had been made. Ten years had been more than enough time to see many other "revolutionary" engines from birth to death, but the Wankel seemed to be thriving. The license purchases convinced the world that the technology was sound and that it was not just another "dream" motor. But the major American companies still had not joined the club, and much of the rest of the world was waiting for them to jump in before making a commitment of their own.

With ample numbers of Prinz Wankels and about 3,000 Spiders on the road, NSU was ready to develop an entirely new car around the Wankel engine. Aware that the Prinz and the Spider could easily be dismissed as "toy" cars, NSU wanted to build a full sized car to enter the market dominated by BMW and Mercedes-Benz. They had been continuing to test and evaluate their engines in highway use and, with money in their corporate pockets from the sale of Wankel licenses to other companies, they set out to design and build a car intended to compete with automobiles like the Mercedes 250S and the BMW 2002.

The NSU RO 80 would be designed around a new twin-rotor engine that was the culmination of everything NSU had learned about making Wankels up to that time. They still placed the intake ports on the periphery, intending to take full advantage of the better breathing characteristics in spite of a little unsteadiness at low engine speeds. But they changed the material of the housings and apex seals. The carbon-aluminum seals of the earlier engines broke easily and often, so now they were changed to cast iron. To give the iron seals a smoother ride, the surface of the aluminum housings was Nicasil, the same material that Mercedes had settled on for its rotor housings. Like the Japanese engines, the RO 80 engine had two sparkplugs per rotor and two independent ignition systems to take advantage of the different optimum sparkplug locations associated with operation at different speeds.

The engine was not the only leading technology to be found in the RO 80. The car had front wheel drive long before it was fashionable, four wheel disk brakes using two calipers on each front disk, and a suspension load proportioning valve to prevent rear-wheel lockup under hard braking. This was at a time when the few cars with disks generally had them only on the front. The car also had an interesting semi-automatic transmission that would shift like a manual, but had no clutch pedal on the floor. Power was run through a torque converter, like an automatic, then through a clutch with an automatic operating mechanism that disengaged the clutch when the driver grabbed the gear lever to shift. The presence of the torque converter in the driveline had

Figure 44. Rotary cars of the 1960s, gathered outside Curtiss-Wright's Rotary Engine Division: NSU RO 80, 1965 Ford Mustang test car, Mazda RX-2 sedan and coupe, Mazda 110S Cosmo.

the added effect of smoothing out the unsteady idle that was a trade-off characteristic of an engine with peripheral intake ports.

Body styling was drawn with aerodynamic drag in mind and designers took advantage of the Wankel engine's low profile to give the car a very low, sloping hood line. Much attention was paid to visibility for passengers as well as the driver, who enjoyed a very large windshield for the size of the car. Extensive wind tunnel testing was done to insure low drag and good stability at high speeds as the RO 80 would be expected to cruise on European roads at speeds over 100 miles per hour.

The RO 80 was unveiled at the Frankfurt auto show in the fall of 1967. The company announced that it expected to go into production at a rate of 50 cars per day on October 1. Along with the German market, they had hoped that the car would sell in Italy, which was already a strong market for NSU's conventional cars. At the time NSU announced no plans to export to the United States. Because of looming air pollution standards, the United States market was a very unpredictable place for a new car with such unusual technology.

When the RO 80 was introduced it was well received for more than its unusual engine. There was a level of quality to the car that was far beyond what anyone had expected from a maker that had been producing small and inexpensive cars for so long. Clearly the company had high aspirations for the new model. The styling was modern, aerodynamic, but conservative as well. The car was large and comfortable compared to NSU's earlier efforts, and it had the Wankel rotary which ran like nothing else in the world.

Introducing the new engine in such an upscale but conservative package was well advised for NSU. The company's earlier experience with the Wankel had shown that the public will turn out in droves to examine a curious new engine, but when it's time to put up the cash, they suddenly become very traditional. By building a car that embraced all of the new technology of the decade and displaying it with obvious craftmanship, NSU appealed to the closet car enthusiast who considered himself to be a progressive thinker.

7

Fichtel and Sachs
Air-Cooled Wankel

Fichtel and Sachs AG is a German company that was a favorite target of Allied bombers during World War II because of its precision ball bearing manufacturing facilities. In 1960 it became the second company to buy a license to produce Wankel engines, acquiring rights for industrial applications in the .5 to 12 horsepower range. In early 1965, they became the first of the Wankel licensees to go into commercial production. While Curtiss-Wright and Toyo Kogyo had built and tested thousands of engines by 1965, all of their engines had been built for the purpose of research and development. Neither had gone into mass production for the purpose of marketing.[1]

The Fichtel and Sachs engine, designated the KM37, was a 108cc engine with an 8.5:1 compression ratio. Its power output was 6.5 horsepower at 5500 rpm. It was an air-cooled engine, compact in size at 8.66 inches high, 11.2 inches wide and 16.5 inches long. That and its light weight (30.5 pounds) made it a very useful powerplant for water pumps, generators, and small recreational vehicles.

Designing a successful air cooled Wankel is especially tricky because of the need to cool the rotor. Most designs for an air cooled Wankel involve an oil cooled rotor and an oil cooler. Fichtel and Sachs' key to developing a useful air-cooled engine without oil cooling the rotor was an arrangement for introducing the cool intake charge through the rotor. The principle was similar to Wankel's DKM125 in that the incoming charge must pass through a transfer port in the rotor, through the rotor, and out another side port. The charge then passed through a channel in the side housing, and through the actual induction port into the rotor chamber.

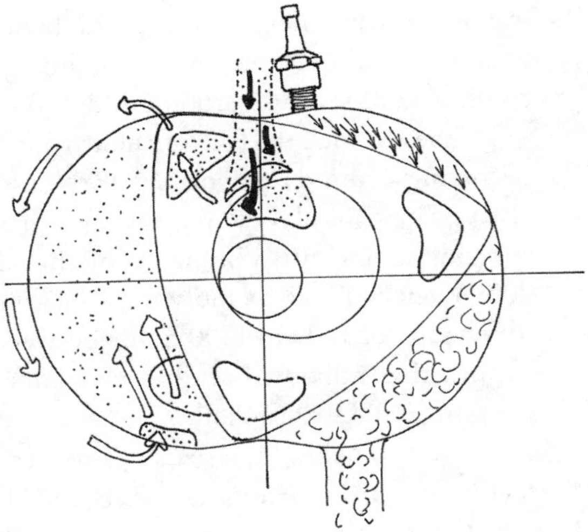

While making this journey, the incoming charge picked up about 50 degrees centigrade in temperature, representing excess heat taken away from the engine. But this heated charge also had the effect of reducing the volumetric efficiency of the engine. Normally this would be considered undesirable, but in this specific application the Fichtel and Sachs engineers depended on this principle to govern the power output and thereby help to keep the operating temperatures down to a level where air cooling was effective.

Figure 45. Fichtel and Sachs kept the rotor in their air-cooled engine cool by passing the incoming charge through it, much like the intake cycle of the DKM 125. The intake charge entered through ports in the side of the engine. It passed through transfer ports in the rotor to the rotor's interior, then back out again, through the other side, picking up heat along the way. The charge then entered the engine through side ports in the normal fashion.

While on Wankel's DKM125 the charge came in through the center shaft, the KM37 drew it in through a port in the side cover which passed the hot side of the epitrochoidal housing, further taking advantage of cooling effects of the charge. Using the charge cooling to supplement the forced air cooling on the hot side of the engine helped keep the heat distribution more even on the rotor housing.

The end covers and epitrochoidal housing center section were cooled by forced air via a shrouded axial flow fan fixed to one end of the shaft. The forced air and induction cooling system kept the temperature of the housing down to around 200 degrees centigrade while the engine was running at maximum load at 6000 rpm. This temperature was similar to an air-cooled piston engine of similar output.

Like a typical two-stroke piston engine, the KM37 was lubricated by mixing oil with the gasoline. Fichtel and Sachs called for a mixture of 2 percent oil by volume and warned against getting the mixture too strong, which could lead to serious carbon buildup on the rotor.

The working surface of the trochoid housing was chrome plated, as was becoming common among Wankel builders at the time. But while everyone else was using molybdenum spray on their side covers, Fichtel and Sachs were spraying theirs with a bronze alloy that they said wore as well, and cost about 20 percent as much as molybdenum. They used cast iron seals and claimed a service life of 1000 to 1200 hours between overhauls. Light springs were used behind the individual sealing elements to keep up the seal contact during cranking, true to Wankel's practice. Once the engine was running, gas pressure directed behind the seals by grooves cut in the seal itself maintained contact between the sealing elements and the rotor housing.

Operating speed proved to be an important factor in the life of the working surface of the housing, as Fichtel and Sachs were having trouble with chatter marks just like everyone else. They found that an engine run at 3000 rpm would go 1500 hours before the surface was damaged, but if the engine were run at 4500 rpm, chatter marks would form after only 1000 hours.

One of the more visible companies to buy the KM37 was Arctic Cat Snowmobiles. Another used the KM37 on a portable firepump. Fichtel and

The first production motorcycle with a Wankel engine: the Hercules W 2000 with 294 cc and 27 HP.

Figure 46. The Hercules W2000 motorcycle used a 27HP Fichtel and Sachs rotary engine.

Sachs later updated their contract with NSU to build larger engines and did build a 20 horsepower, 303cc unit called the KM914 for the German Hercules motorcycle.

Hercules motorcycles were built by the German DKW motorcycle works, which had become part of the Sachs group. The Hercules rotary motorcycle, dubbed the W 2000, appeared on the scene at a motorcycle trade show in Germany in 1970, but it wasn't until 1973 that the company built 50 bikes for introduction to dealers. Later, in 1974, production began on a large scale and motorcycles were built for export as well as for domestic sale.

Performance of the W2000 was not particularly strong—top speed was not quite 90 mph—so the bike's biggest selling point was its novelty, as would be the case with many rotary engined vehicles. Eventually, the company built over 1800 W 2000 motorcycles before halting production and selling the tooling to Norton Motorcycles in England. Norton would eventually build several of its own versions of the Wankel and would continue to produce them in motorcycles for many years.

8

Citroën

Citroën, the second largest French automobile company, built a wide range of cars from spacious luxury sedans (the "D" models) to the 2CV, a tiny and very basic economy car built to make automotive transportation available to everyone. All Citroëns were front wheel drive long before it became popular in the rest of the world. Most people in the United States remember Citroën as the "car that went up and down" as the upper line cars were built around an air over hydraulic suspension system in which the car was "sprung" on pressurized nitrogen contained at about 800 psi in accumulator spheres at each corner. Attached to each sphere was a hydraulic cylinder pressurized by an engine-driven pump. The sphere-cylinder assembly took the place of a conventional spring and shock absorber. Ride height was controlled by the volume of fluid in the cylinder and could be adjusted by the driver from the driver's seat. Any movement of the suspension forced fluid through a series of dampening valves into the bottom of the sphere, compressing the nitrogen gas on the other side of a diaphragm, giving a spring like action that had a low tendency to oscillate. The total effect was a car with an amazingly smooth ride that handled well (though body roll was high) and could run well on virtually any road surface.

At the time of the Wankel's invention, Citroën was run by Pierre Bercot. Bercot was a tough businessman, like many of the people involved in the Wankel story, who ran his company from the top and kept his own counsel.

He was interested in applying technical innovation to his cars, as shown in his products right up to the 1955 introduction of the DS model, so the company was truly a natural to consider building Wankel powered automobiles.

Bercot sent Andre Noel, a representative who had dealt with NSU in the past on Citroën's behalf, to meet with von Heydekampf, but he was told that he could not have an engine unless he bought a license first.

Bercot was soon introduced to Max Bunford by a mutual friend. Bunford held a major share of NSU stock, having inherited some and bought more shortly after the war when stock in most German companies was considered worthless. Bunford had a vision of a united Europe, and working around the Wankel engine, he hoped to build NSU into a major European automobile company.

Citroën and Bunford held meetings with NSU to discuss how the Wankel could be developed to their mutual benefit, and in 1964 formed a company, Société d'Étude Comobile. The purpose of the new company was to explore and develop ways to market an automobile using an NSU Wankel engine and a car built by Citroën. Comobile would employ members of the technical and marketing staffs from both NSU and Citroën. The company was to study markets, make proposals for and produce designs for a jointly produced car. To quote Bunford, "NSU would produce the most extraordinary engines to match the extraordinary cars made by Citroën."[1]

Citroën and NSU formed another company together in 1967, the Compagnie Europeenne de Construction de Moteurs Automobiles or Comotor SA. Comotor, initially capitalized at $1 million, was intended to construct and market Wankel engines for any and all applications and to manufacture the appropriate accessories for these applications. The board of directors in several sessions raised the capital to $4.04 million and in 1969 Comotor purchased a site for construction of an engine assembly plant in the Saar region of West Germany with plans for completion in 1970.

Meanwhile, the product of Comobile's labor, the Citroën M35, was announced. The M35 was an experimental car, though it was meant to be sold to the general public. Citroën felt that the best way to research the behavior of the Wankel under a variety of conditions was to sell it, where the buying public would test it in ways that only the buying public can. Citroën was not at all hasty about getting into Wankel production, however, preferring to ease into it very slowly. Production of the M35 was to begin with only 500 cars to be sold in the French domestic market. They hoped later to be able to evaluate the cars in 1974 before committing to production. By guaranteeing the engine for two years with no mileage limit, Citroën felt that they could

Figure 47. The Citroën M35 single rotor car using the Comotor KKM613 engine.

ensure that most of the cars sold would be back for evaluation after their experience in the real world.

The engine built by NSU for the M35 was designated the KKM 613. It was based on the old KKM 502 design which was the engine in the NSU Spider. It was liquid cooled with an oil cooled rotor, with some additional refinements brought in courtesy of research on the RO 80 engine. A heat exchanger had been added to keep the engine oil temperature down. The spark plug openings were given a copper insert to help conduct heat in the spark plug area and minimize thermal loads that were causing cracks in the housing. The housings themselves were coated with a silicone-nickel alloy, like the Nickasil used by Mercedes but under the name of Einisil. The apex seals were made from cast iron in a three-piece configuration and the corner and side seals had been re-designed. Apex seals were lubricated by way of an oil metering system built into the fuel pump.

The Citroën M35 was a small four-seat business coupe. It had front wheel drive, with the single rotor engine hanging out in front. Most of the body parts were lifted off the shelf from the existing Ami8 sedan and the 2CV, which used a horizontally opposed, air cooled, two cylinder engine. With the standard equipment 26 horsepower piston engine, the 2CV and Ami were both painfully slow. At 55 horsepower and 50.6 lb ft of torque, the NSU Wankel was a big improvement. It was given new transmission ratios to make it more compatible with the new engine, and enabling it to reach 80 mph in third gear if necessary to maintain speed. The indicated maximum revolutions were 7500 rpm on the tachometer, and a buzzer was added because the new engine was so easy to rev.

Though the M35 was not considered to be a high-end car, it was equipped with the Hydropneumatic suspension that had made Citroën famous for its comfortable ride. The sphere-cylinder assemblies were fitted to the same suspension arms used on the 2CV Dyane in place of the coil springs.[2]

The M35 was not intended to be a large scale production car, but was designed and constructed completely for research and development purposes. Citroën meant to produce 500 of the cars, but ultimately produced only about 250. Citroën would produce a Wankel car, but it would be a luxury car with a larger, twin-rotor engine built by Comotor.

The Comotor engine was based on the KKM 612 engine built by NSU for the RO 80, and was designated the KKM 624. It used the latest nickel-silicone surface for the rotor housing as well as cast iron apex seals in iron rotors. It produced 107 horsepower at 6500 rpm and 101 foot pounds of torque at 3000, enough to drive its host car to a top speed of 110 mph. Like the RO 80, the Comotor engine had peripheral intake ports, but it had single spark-plugs instead of the two per rotor of the NSU engine.

Comotor placed its bet for building a good engine on precision assembly techniques. Using a lesson learned by Citroën in the construction of its hydropneumatic suspension systems, manufacturing facilities were kept meticulously clean, with parts washing stations employed between each stage of machining operations to remove all of the debris resulting from the machining. Then, before final assembly, all parts for the engine underwent an ultrasonic cleaning process.[3]

Rotors were classified by weight in a margin of 20 grams. Only rotors in the

Figure 48. Cross section of the KKM624 engine for the Citroën GS Birotor.

Figure 49, *top.* **The GS Birotor subframe assembly. Figure 50,** *bottom.* **The ambitious but unsuccessful Citroën GS Birotor.**

same weight class could go into the same engine. Apex seals were made in eight different lengths, varying by a few ten-thousandths of an inch, so that the engine assembler could select the perfect size seal within a very narrow tolerance.

Comotor had hoped to sell twin rotor engines to auto manufacturers other than Citroën. There was talk by now of the whole world converting over to Wankel power someday, and buying a ready made unit from Comotor could be a lot cheaper than developing a Wankel independently. But the precision assembly system had the undesired side effect of making the engine very expensive which probably drove other manufacturers away from the Comotor option. The price of a bare engine was not disclosed, but the Twin Rotor GS itself sold for $4500, which by 1974 standards, made it a very high priced car.

The Citroën GS rotary was an upscale car for the high-end market. It was targeted at the same market as NSU's RO 80 models as a very sophisticated and advanced four-door sport sedan. The engine was mounted transversely over the front axle and paired with a semiautomatic three-speed transmission, another feature of the RO 80. The transmission was made by Citroën. It was manually shifted but used an automatic clutch and a torque converter to smooth out the shifts.

Unfortunately, the GS was a failure. Few cars were ever built, only about 850 in all. Most were recalled and destroyed by Citroën. The Comotor twin rotor did not live up to its promise of durability and was troubled by breakage of the apex seals and engine seizure, problems that would also haunt the RO 80. But Citroën continued to sell a version of the GS powered by a conventional engine. Other rotary efforts were planned but never gelled as relations between Citroën and NSU had gone downhill through the 1960s. For a while, there was talk of an actual merger, as both companies had needed a partner to strengthen their financial positions. But it was Fiat in 1968 that eventually bought a stake in Citroën from the Michelin family who controlled it, and NSU lost all interest.

9

The Wankel at Daimler-Benz

Wankel's earlier work on military projects left him with a few important contacts including Wolf Dieter Bensinger, who had been working with Daimler-Benz since the war. Bensinger had been assigned to develop new engines for passenger cars and was responsible for the line of six-cylinder overhead camshaft engines that Mercedes put in the 220 series cars in the 1950s. He had worked with Wankel during the war on the rotary valve engine projects and followed his work at NSU as his new engine was beginning to take shape. In 1960 he went to visit Wankel to discuss the possibility of developing a rotary engine to replace the existing Mercedes overhead cam six cylinder.

Wankel and Bensinger made a gentlemen's agreement. There was no license sold and no money changed hands at first. Bensinger wanted to be able to study the engine and make a case for or against it to the management before the company invested large sums of money. NSU provided Daimler-Benz with test engines, and Daimler-Benz would share any knowledge that they acquired during testing and development. After spending some time evaluating the engine, Bensinger sent a report on the potential of the Wankel to the president of the company, Walter Hitzinger, and Hitzinger decided to negotiate a legal contract with NSU for Wankel rights.

Hitzinger dragged negotiations out and repeatedly stalled signing, possibly because the industrialist Dr. Friedrich Flick, the controlling stock-holder at Daimler-Benz, was buying up NSU stock at every chance. If he were able to gain control of NSU, Mercedes could build Wankels without ever having to buy a license. But eventually it became clear that ownership of NSU would be a long time coming, if at all, and Hitzinger settled negotiations, buying a license giving them the right to build gasoline powered Wankel engines of 50 horsepower and above for $750,000 to be paid in three annual installments. The agreement was signed in October of 1961 and included an annual minimum payment to NSU and Wankel GmBH. The payment was designed to see that companies buying Wankel technology would work to develop it quickly in order to begin to recoup their investment. Later, in March of 1964, Daimler-Benz obtained a license to produce any size diesel Wankel engine. Whether or not any plans existed to produce such engines at that time, the agreement was considered necessary insurance against the company's suffering from technical obsolescence, should the rest of the world adopt the Wankel as its preferred powerplant.

Bensinger had begun his research program in 1960, long before the agreement was reached between the two companies. His position in the company was strong enough that he didn't always have to go through official channels to conduct work on something he considered promising. He wanted to develop a single rotor 700cc engine and a 1400cc twin rotor version simultaneously. His engines were like NSU's in that they were water cooled with oil cooled rotors and had peripheral intake ports. The engines did well at first, the twin rotor developing 170 horsepower when new, but the engine's life span was short. Initially, Bensinger's test programs went much like Wankel research programs in other parts of the world: his engines would run well for 400 hours or so and then the power would begin to fall off. Disassembling the engines inevitably showed seal chatter marks forming on the surface of the trochoidal housing.

Bensinger's explanation of the formation of the chatter marks was that during operation, the leading edge seal would push oil, carbon, combustion byproducts and fuel ahead of itself. When these substances built up and the resistance got too high, the seal would lift over the pile and off the working surface of the housing. When the trailing edge of the seal would strike the surface again, it would break small particles off of the working surface. It was the same old problem with a different theory. But just as everywhere else, the solution would have to be found in the seal and housing materials.

While working on rotor cooling systems, Bensinger found that the cooling oil inside NSU's rotor design did not always move in a predictable fashion.

In some places it might be stagnant; in others it would foam. One solution considered was to close the cavities at the tips of the rotors and fill them with liquid sodium, a remarkably efficient conductor of heat. Makers of high performance engines had been using sodium cooled exhaust valves for years. But sodium filled rotors would be very expensive indeed, even by Mercedes standards. So the design concentration was to improve oil circulation inside the rotor, on the belief that when this was achieved, the sodium cooled tips would be unnecessary.

The successful design of the rotor interior used the washing machine agitator–like motion of the rotor to swirl the cooling oil in the three individual cavities. Oil for lubricating the bearings was leaked to the rotor cavity where it swirled around the interior wall of the rotor face. When the movement of the oil forced it towards the shaft, a port in the rotor lined up with a port on the shaft and the oil was allowed to escape the rotor and eventually to drain back to the sump.

Of course, as with all other Wankel researchers, Bensinger experienced problems with the life of the apex seals. His experiments covered different materials, but he also made an intense study of the dynamics of the combustion process in the engine to see, among other things, just what sort of conditions the seals had to endure.

What he found was that the shape of the combustion chambers in the Wankel produced an extraordinarily high gas velocity in the engine. The gas velocity was so high in fact that under some conditions it even outran the advance of the flame front. The result was that the flame front did not reach the apex seals until the temperature and pressure of combustion had fallen off considerably. As the rotor face passed the minor axis, the gas was forced forward with such speed that the flame front was always working to catch up. After ignition, the trailing side of the flame front stayed essentially at the minor axis and the trailing apex seal swept the unburnt gas to it. The leading side of the flame front followed the apex seal, reaching it well after peak. This meant that the apex seals stayed relatively cool, so they could be made of materials that had low resistance to heat.

Bensinger made his experimental seals out of carbon and aluminum. In testing, they were able to achieve a seal life of about 60,000 miles of driving before the seals were worn enough to cause starting problems. Matters were worse when the driving consisted of short trips with many stops and starts, the most common type of automotive use, as excess gasoline from cold starts and other low speed driving conditions would wash the oil film off of the working surface. A useful life of 60,000 miles might have been acceptable endurance for a minicar like the NSU Prinz or the Spider, but it was just a starting point for Mercedes, a company with a reputation for building cars for the long haul.

It was the head of Daimler's newly founded rotary department, Dr. Heinz Lamm, who found a truly successful material for the apex seals and rotor housings. He rejected outright NSU's choice of soft carbon materials against a hard chromium surface and instead looked for two compatible hard surfaces. The material that he finally settled on as most appropriate for the rotor housings was an alloy of nickel and silicone carbide developed by Mahle Kolbenwerk specifically for Daimler-Benz. NSU later took it up as did many other Wankel licensees.

Having chosen what he felt was the best rotor housing surface available, Lamm set to finding a compatible material for the apex seals. He tried some ceramic materials, and even quartz. He even tried using a composite of some powder that he scraped from an air extractor vent of a grinding company in Augsburg. Such was the nature of the study of possible seal materials: Nothing could be ignored. Even the most outrageous notions had to be studied just in case they turned out to be the winning combination.

Lamm found what he wanted at Rolls-Royce. Rolls-Royce was working on a diesel Wankel and had developed a seal for that engine from a then-new material, a ceramic form of silicone carbide. It was an excellent material, and a perfect match for the Nickasil surface, but it was very expensive. Enough material to make up the seals for one twin-rotor engine cost about $20. This of course wasn't a problem for Daimler-Benz, who were in the business of producing high end cars, but when NSU tried to buy the material, they found the asking price too high and refused to buy it.[1]

Some experiments were done with a system that used a seal set in a steel insert that rested in the rotor, an arrangement considered but rejected at Curtiss-Wright. Designers claimed that the system made it possible to use thinner seals, which could better conform to minute variations in the working surface. But tests showed that it lasted no longer than the wider conventional seals mounted directly in the rotor.

Bensinger devoted much study to various methods for distributing oil into the engine for lubricating the rotor tips. NSU had been mixing oil with the fuel, but Bensinger decided that this method was too inconsistent to be reliable. He wanted the oil introduced into the intake stream to be precisely controlled—just enough to enhance the seal at the rotor tips, no more or less. The first patented method involved a metallic wick in the intake airstream. Oil was metered to the wick by a sort of rotating valve driven at rotor speed.

The valve consisted of a drilling in a shaft that contained a small pin. The pin was allowed to move slightly inside its little cylinder, just enough to admit a small quantity of oil at either end. The shaft rotated in a housing that had two ports to line up with the drilling, one connected to the oiling system, and one connected to a reservoir leading to the oil wick. When the drillings lined up with the ports, oil was pumped into one end and the movement of the pin pushed the oil contained in the other side of the drilling into the reservoir leading to the wick. The process was repeated each time the shaft rotated 180 degrees. This system closely regulated the oil fed into the engine, keeping it consistently proportional to rotor speed, regardless of oil pressure.

The next development for oiling the seals involved sleeves in the intakes that had cavities which held oil over a large area around the sleeve, fed by their own oil pump. The idea behind the sleeves was to keep the oil from entering the engine in the center of the airstream where it would be burned with the mixture. Rather, it was kept to the outer sides of the incoming airstream where it would reach the metal surfaces and the apex seals.

Mercedes' first experimental Wankels were carbureted, like those in most other test labs around the world. But after exhaustive testing, it was decided that fuel-injection would be most appropriate for the Wankel, mostly because of the engine's low thermal efficiency. The thermal efficiency of a Wankel is low partly because of its relatively slow combustion, and partly because of the large surface area to volume ratio. The Wankel has large flat end housings and the outer trochoid housing, all of which are water cooled and provide a surface on which fuel droplets can condense when the engine is fed fuel vapor in an ordinary fashion by a carburetor. These surfaces also soak up heat from combustion, lowering the specific power output of the engine.

Erratic driving characteristics are sometimes brought on by the same conditions that reduce the engine's thermal efficiency. The low turbulence of the intake air on a Wankel, combined with the large surface area of the inside of the engine, could store large amounts of condensed fuel at low throttle openings. The engine would continue to draw in a certain amount of fuel, along with exhaust from the previous combustion cycle. When the throttle opening was suddenly decreased, as happens frequently in normal driving, the engine might lurch suddenly several times before stabilizing. Fuel injection would solve this and other drivability problems by more thoroughly atomizing fuel, more precisely metering it to the engine, directing it into the engine exactly where the designer wanted it, and by shutting it off when it was not needed.

Mercedes had been a pioneer in the field of fuel injection systems for passenger cars for years. While they had been making diesels, they had also been developing gasoline injection pumps based on some of the diesel pump designs. By the time the Wankel was under development, Mercedes already had several proven gasoline injection systems in production, some using port injection, where the fuel is sprayed onto the back side of the intake valve, and some using direct injection, spraying the fuel under high pressure directly into the combustion chamber itself. Adapting existing systems to the Wankel was not a big challenge, but the placement of the injectors themselves took a lot of experimentation. The options for injector placement on a piston engine are fairly limited, but the Wankel has half a rotor housing to consider in searching for the optimum location.

While researching methods of fuel injection for the Wankel, engineers took out several patents. One taken by Heinz Lamm and Willi Springer dealt with injecting fuel in a narrow stream directly at the cavity in the face of the rotor. By spraying the fuel directly into the area of the highest air velocity, they hoped to take advantage of what turbulence there was in the chamber of the Wankel. They claimed that their method had all the advantages of direct injection, without the disadvantages associated with locating an injector directly in the housing such as a gap in the compression seal where the injector opening was and interfering with the passage of coolant around the hot side of the housing. Another patent involved a piece of sheetmetal wound into a helix and placed in the intake port, where the fuel was sprayed down its length. Supposedly, this would increase the turbulence of the mixture entering the engine. Niether approach went very far with Bensinger.

Bensinger liked direct injection for the Wankel. He wanted to use it because it would enable the application of a method called "stratified charge." A statified charge occurs when, by accident or design, the fuel mix in the combustion chamber forms up in rich and lean layers, the rich mix making up a very small percentage of the charge volume. The rich mixture is ignited by a sparkplug, and the lean portion is ignited by the heat of the rich mixture burning. This enables the designer to run far leaner overall fuel mixtures than with conventionally aspirated engines.

Working with an engineer named Friedrich Nallinger, Bensinger developed a direct injection system that employed two sparkplugs and a single injector which was aimed roughly toward the sparkplugs. The fuel was to be injected during the last half of the intake phase where they hoped it would fill the combustion chamber at the portion near the sparkplugs right at the moment of ignition. From that point, they reasoned that the rotor would sweep the lean mixture toward the burning rich mix. The second sparkplug was

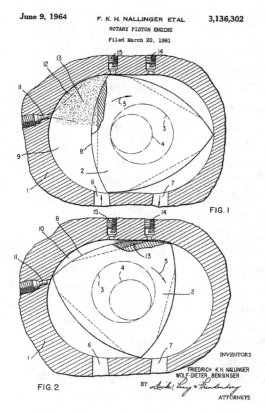

June 9, 1964   F. K. H. NALLINGER ETAL   3,136,302
ROTARY PISTON ENGINE
Filed March 20, 1961

FIG. 1

INVENTORS
FRIEDRICH K.H. NALLINGER
WOLF-DIETER BENSINGER
BY
ATTORNEYS

FIG. 2

Patent drawings of Friedrich Nallinger's stratified charge system.

intended to fire late in the combustion phase and was located above the minor axis where it would be able to fire off any combustible end-gas.

In theory it looked good. Then they discovered that the only advancing flame front in a working Wankel was on the leading side of the chamber, chasing the leading edge of the rotor toward the exhaust port. Their design had counted on a flame front moving counter to the direction of the rotor to ignite the leaner portion of the charge, and the engine just didn't work that way.

Another engineer, Hans Scherenberg, began to draw different proposed direct injection systems for achieving stratified charge in the Wankel. Most of his proposals involved the use of two injectors per rotor pointed roughly toward each other. By varying the relative quantities injected by the two different injectors, Scherenberg could achieve nearly any degree of stratification he wanted under a variety of running conditions. During low load conditions, one injector could be shut off completely so that high pressure could be maintained at low fuel volume. This system would permit the flexibility to cope with upcoming U.S. exhaust emission regulations.

In 1966, Mercedes was testing a 1.8 liter twin-rotor engine designed specifically for passenger cars. Shortly thereafter, a third rotor was added making it a 2.7 liter. And in 1967 a larger, 3.3 liter three-rotor was built with the U.S. emission regulations in mind. This engine was lengthened a little to increase the rotor width by 5 millimeters, raising the displacement to 3.6 liters. This would be Mercedes' most famous Wankel, the C111.[2]

NSU realized early on that the Wankel was well suited for high performance applications, especially with the peripheral intake port layout. With volumetric efficiency reaching over 100 percent, a Wankel rotary could pass quite a lot of fuel through itself, even if it could not burn it all in the process. NSU chose a sports car for its rotary, and so did Mercedes-Benz.

The C111 was an exercise by all the styling and experimental departments at Daimler. It was a project conceived by Rudolf Uhlenhaut, the chief of passenger car development. Uhlenhaut was a big fan of racing and had been instrumental in the design of Mercedes' race cars from 1937 to 1954. Frustrated with Mercedes' decision to withdraw from racing after 1955, he was eager for an opportunity to build an exciting car again. Uhlenhaut worked with Hans Scherenberg and Ludwig Kraus to persuade the board of directors that the best way to pursue development of the Wankel's potential and simultaneously to work on a new semi-trailing arm rear axle design would be to build a high performance GT car prototype. The car would be built to use a high-performance version of Mercedes' V8, or a three or four rotor Wankel engine mounted ahead of the rear axle centerline, the new semi-trailing arm suspension, and a body of plastic composite to study its potential for use in future production cars.

The plan was for the body proper to be made of plastic and attached to the steel platform, but the engineering department had the platform ready well before the first plastic body was complete. The engineers were anxious to try it out, so they built their own body out of sheets of aluminum to enable them to begin tests. Their body only slightly resembled the intended shape of the car, but it served its purpose and they commenced testing. They quickly discovered that the semi-trailing arm suspension did not have the straight line stability they needed at the speeds of which the C111 was capable so it was abandoned in favor of a double wishbone type suspension of a kind more common to open-wheeled race cars. The front suspension was a wishbone system with an unusually high upper link, a system that strongly resembled the suspension used in the front of Mercedes' large sedans built in the 1980s and early 1990s.

The car first appeared at the 1969 Frankfurt auto show as the C101, and was billed to be an experimental prototype of a car that Mercedes was considering for moving into the markets served by the likes of Porsche, Ferrari, and Lamborghini. The real body was styled by Karl Wilfert, the man responsible for the 300SL gullwing coupe. Its unit body construction was like a Can-Am car for the street. It was wide and low, with a deep tub for the driver and passenger flanked by two 16 gallon fuel tanks built into the wide door sills. The doors opened straight up, gull-wing style, invoking memories of the 300SL. The first real body was an improvement over the engineers' makeshift model, but as in many first edition exotic cars, visibility was poor, the cooling ducts worked poorly and it just wasn't very graceful looking. But as wind tunnel testing continued, it was reshaped and evolved into the Mark II version, acquiring a sleek and refined look. Cooling ducts were moved, the windshield was made larger and the dashboard lowered, and the rear of the car was redesigned to improve visibility.[3]

Mounted in the middle of the car, behind the driver and ahead of the rear axle line, the three rotor Wankel engine really made the car. Making 330 horsepower and weighing only 308 pounds, the engine weighed about half as much as a conventional V-8 of similar output. The high power to weight ratio of the car gave it a 0 to 60 capability of 4.9 seconds, 0 to 100 of 14.9. The engine used mechanical fuel injection with two injectors for each rotor located at different points on the periphery of the housing. The injection pump was driven off of a shaft which also drove the oil metering pump and distributor drive. The ignition was by a single, surface-gap sparkplug fired by a transistorized ignition system.

The three-rotor cars were said to have a top speed of over 170 mph. Later, Mercedes built a four-rotor engine and installed it in some of the cars. The first of the C111 MKII's four-rotor cars had 70 more horsepower and were reported to be capable of over 180 mph. The automotive journalists loved the car, and it became a regular feature on the European auto show circuit. But

Figure 52. The Mercedes-Benz C111: 1969 version (left) and 1970 version (right).

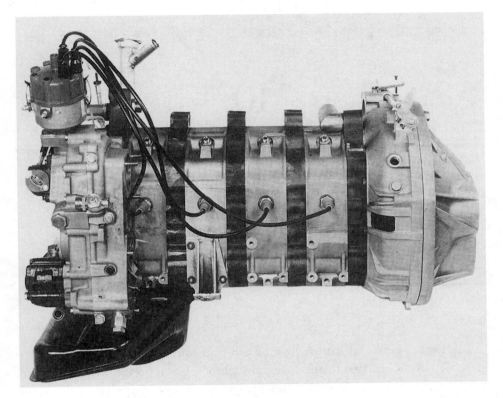

Figure 53. The four rotor engine of the C111 produced nearly 400 horsepower.

while Mercedes denied that they were preparing to go racing, they would not give a straight answer as to future plans for the car or the Wankel in general.

Several blank checks arrived from potential buyers who wanted to be among the first to own a C111 should they go into production, but those people were disappointed.

In the C111 Mercedes had a fairly reliable Wankel engine, one powerful enough to drive the large sedans that they specialized in producing. But the unknown (for 1969 anyway) factor was the looming specter of exhaust emission regulation in the United States.

The United States was a big market for Mercedes and getting much bigger. The question of whether their Wankel engines could be made clean enough to be sold in America was still unanswered, and to commit to producing Wankel engines this late in the game might be unwise. After having made major progress over a few years, achieving reliable injection systems and longer lasting seals Mercedes seemed content to let the rotary remain a laboratory toy for a while.

10

Rolls-Royce and the Diesel Wankel

Diesel engines, which use heat of compression to ignite a heavy oil fuel, generally use about two thirds as much fuel for a given power output as their gasoline powered counterparts. Always popular in heavy equipment and trucks, they were out of favor in passenger cars during the 1960s and '70s because of their greater weight, noise and vibration than a gasoline engine. The Wankel was an interesting candidate for diesel development as it presented the possibility of overcoming some of the diesel's more objectionable qualities. If a suitable diesel Wankel could be developed, it would in theory be lighter, quieter and smoother than a reciprocating version, and possibly the diesel's advantage in fuel economy could offset the Wankel's relatively thirsty nature.

As mentioned, Curtiss-Wright spent a good deal of effort working on a "heavy fuel" engine, meaning an engine that would run on heavier oil distillates like diesel fuel or jet fuel, but their design used spark ignition and had a relatively low compression ratio. So even though it burned diesel fuel, it was not a diesel engine proper.

Rolls-Royce, the British firm well known for its extraordinarily expensive luxury automobiles, preferred by royalty and overpaid entertainers, is less well known to automobile enthusiasts for its aircraft engine and diesel truck engine divisions that actually support the company. Normally, Rolls-Royce maintained a reputation as a deeply conservative engineering firm, not given to innovation but supplying extremely reliable products by making use of proven technology and devoting meticulous attention to detail. During the 1960s, however, the company was dominated by headstrong and adventurous engineers who were eager to try out new technology, and because of their connections, they were able to get the British military to support much of their research.

A Rolls-Royce technical advisor brought a Wankel engine to the lab and showed it to the chief executive, Sir Denning Pearson, who in turn showed it to Fritz Feller, a young engineer who was then working on building a multi-fuel engine for tanks and military trucks. Multi-fuel capability meant that any available fuel from jet fuel to gasoline could be used. It was considered a useful quality in a military vehicle where supplies of any given type of fuel could be interrupted at any moment. Also, military vehicles with multi-fuel capability could more easily make use of captured fuel supplies during wartime. Pearson and Feller recognized that, because of its high power to weight ratio, a Wankel rotary diesel would be an ideal candidate for study, particularly as an engine for air-transported vehicles.

Rolls obtained a license to produce Wankel diesels in 1965. Negotiations were not easy as the Germans in the "Diesel Club"—truck manufacturers MAN Krupp, Klockner Humbolt Deutz, and Daimler-Benz—were not interested in admitting Rolls-Royce and sharing their technology. They had all taken out licenses and intended to share their new technology as it developed. Although they had done very little development work of their own, they were not convinced that the British firm would come up with anything of substance to add to the general body of knowledge that they had accumulated on diesel engines. The normally genteel British representatives were caught unprepared for the negotiating style of the Germans, and suffered some embarrassment as a bargaining session in a British country inn turned into a shouting match between two of the German negotiators. Nevertheless, the British were eventually able to obtain a specialized license to produce engines from 100 to 850 horsepower.[1]

Using spark ignition and direct fuel injection, Mercedes and Curtiss-Wright had built engines that ran well on diesel fuel, but Rolls-Royce wanted to build a proper diesel working with compression ignition and the extremely high pressures that were involved. Analysis of rotor shapes and eccentricity ratios showed that using the large K factor necessary to obtain diesel-like compression ratios resulted in a very large Wankel indeed. So Rolls-Royce

Jan. 11, 1966   F. FELLER   3,228,183
                ROTARY INTERNAL COMBUSTION ENGINE
Filed Jan. 20, 1964   5 Sheets-Sheet 1

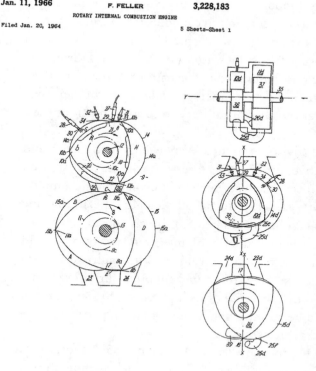

Figure 54. Patent drawing of Feller's compound rotary diesel. The smaller structure is the engine itself; the larger is the compressor. The drawings at right show how the two could be arranged side by side on a common shaft for compactness.

settled on a unique solution, stacking two engines on top of one another. The larger of the two was simply an air pump for the smaller, which was the engine itself. This arrangement enabled the smaller unit to achieve diesel compression without employing a high R/E ratio (or K factor) and the problems along with it.

For their early experiments, the Rolls-Royce engineers used NSU engines. They already had plans for the compound engine arrangement that they would later put into practice, but in order to get started on some preliminary research, they simulated the first stage by piping in preheated pressurized air in order to run their NSU Wankel as a diesel. Though they were satisfied with the performance of the side seals at diesel pressures, they found that at high pressures, the apex seals were lifting off of the rotor housing in the area around the point of maximum compression. So the seals were redesigned into an L shape with passages that allowed gas to get behind the seals and force them toward the outer surface.

The revised seals led to a reduction in specific fuel consumption due to the increase in sealing efficiency. Rolls-Royce felt that their new seal design would be helpful in any high performance Wankel application, gas or diesel, where combustion sealing was a problem due to unusually high gas pressures.

Development of the chamber in the face of the rotor was also the subject of much research by Rolls. To achieve the kind of turbulence they wanted for good fuel mixture distribution, they employed the "squish" action that takes place on the trailing face of the rotor as it approaches its closest point to the minor axis. There was a narrow channel cut into the face of the rotor through which the air in the trailing part of the chamber was forced past the minor axis. At the point where the air passed the minor axis, the chamber opened up where curved sides caused it to swirl around the newly injected fuel.

The engine that culminated all of the research done on these subjects would be the 2-R6, a two-rotor engine using two air pumping rotors. The estimated power output was 350 HP at 4500 rpm. Estimated weight of the engine was 929 pounds, about half the weight of a piston type diesel of similar output.

Rolls-Royce was hoping that their rotary diesel would replace conventional diesels in trucks and military equipment during the 1970s. Their competition for the job was considered to be a 350 HP gas turbine engine under development by British Leyland. The Leyland turbine was considerably larger than the Rolls engine, but similar in weight. One advantage that Rolls-Royce saw in the Wankel was that it could be easily built up for a variety of applications. They anticipated designing a four-rotor engine based on the 2-R6 having a projected power output of 700 HP.[2]

Eventually, although Feller's work was proceeding well as he produced larger and larger engines, work was stopped on the engine for financial reasons. The company went bankrupt and Pearson had to resign. The British government picked up the pieces and Rolls-Royce was nationalized. Feller was allowed to continue work on the engine for a while, but it was officially stopped in 1974.[3]

It was speculated that the Yom Kippur War of 1973 changed the future for the Rolls-Royce diesel Wankel. After witnessing the effectiveness of the new portable anti-tank missiles in combat, the British military decided to rethink the role of the airborne tank in combat, and the tanks intended for the Rolls-Royce rotary were dropped from the procurement program.

Whatever the primary reason, the result was the demise of an intriguing Wankel variant.

11

Emissions Regulations and the Wankel

The auto makers knew that restrictions on tailpipe emissions were coming and that when they did, they would severely affect the operations of every auto manufacturer. The idea of the government issuing strict regulations concerning the design of a product manufactured in private industry is just part of our lives now, but in the late 1960s, it was new and some people considered it unjustifiably intrusive.

The state of the environment in the United States was becoming a big political issue. For the hundred or so years since the days of the Industrial Revolution, industries had been disposing of their wastes in essentially whatever fashion was convenient. Factories had been belching smoke into the air and pouring untreated wastes into the rivers in such quantities that the cities in which they operated were rapidly becoming uninhabitable. And of course, increasing numbers of automobiles were driving around these cities making their own enormous contribution to the air pollution problem. Scientists were writing papers and making speeches about the rapidly deteriorating environment. But most importantly, things were bad enough that average people were starting to notice, and to agree that things could not go on forever as they had.

Local governments and some state governments began passing laws regulating the emissions of factories, some requiring sophisticated smoke treatment to reduce or remove the most offensive components. Regulations on the content of industrial wastewater and methods of on-site treatment were studied and some were passed. And automotive exhaust became a subject of intense study for the purpose of initiating emissions standards for future cars.

In 1968 President Nixon appointed an "environmental task force" charged with studying pollution problems and recommending appropriate action. It reported to the president in February 1969 that no sweeping new reforms should take place, but greater effort should be made to enforce any existing regulations and programs. Probably the most significant point was the suggestion that existing programs could be more effective if the administration had a central environmental policy to control and direct the many small agencies scattered about the country each doing its own job in its own way.[1]

In July 1970, Nixon submitted to Congress his plans to establish two new agencies for the purpose of researching and enforcing government environmental policy. They would be the EPA or Environmental Protection Agency, and the NOAA or National Oceanic and Atmospheric Administration. Charged with taking over the air pollution monitoring responsibilities, the EPA would be the agency that most affected the automobile industry.[2] With the passage of the Air Pollution Control Act of 1970, emissions standards for automotive exhaust, present and future, were set. Researchers who had been studying automotive emissions for several years at the behest of several universities had determined that the most harmful components of auto exhaust were unburned hydrocarbons (HC), carbon monoxide (CO) and oxides of nitrogen (NOx). The act provided that carbon monoxide and unburned hydrocarbon content in auto exhaust be reduced, in increasing steps, by 90 percent over prevailing levels in the 1970 models. From 1976 on, the act dictated that nitrogen oxide emissions should be cut by 90 percent over 1971 models.

Auto makers went into an uproar. They complained that the standards were completely impractical. They declared that they had become the national whipping boys for the environmentalists and that the government should apply regulations where they would be more effective. General Motors, Ford, Chrysler, International Harvester, and Volvo all applied to have a year's extension of the standards' deadline, protesting that, despite millions of research dollars spent, they could not bring their car lines into compliance by 1975 with their existing technology. Henry Ford II told stockholders in May of 1972, "If the emission standards are not suspended, the result so far as we can see would be to force suspension of most U.S. automotive manufacturing in 1975." William Ruckelshaus, administrator of the EPA, refused to budge citing several emission control systems that were having good success under laboratory conditions.[3] His opinion was that the automakers would rather spend their time and money in litigation and negotiation than in research and development, and he wanted to send them back to the test labs.

It was ironic that the imposition of automotive emission regulations should bring the Wankel more into focus for the American manufacturers, but that is what happened. Up until now, the Wankel had been considered a relatively "dirty" engine, with HC output nearly three times that of a piston engine. But as many of its inherent problems had been solved by relentless research, those who had invested in the engine had hopes of cleaning it up for use in U.S. autos to come. Charles Jones, chief engineer of Curtiss-Wright's rotary development program, remarked that current rotaries were cleaner without emission controls than conventional engines were in the early 1960s, and he was confident that further study would reduce emissions even further. Having been around for only about 13 years, the Wankel was still in its very early stages of development and the engineers did not have the benefit of years of successes and failures that they enjoyed with conventional engines.

In 1968, in anticipation of coming emissions regulations, Curtiss-Wright engaged Dr. David Cole, a professor of mechanical engineering at the University of Michigan to do an emissions study on the engine.

They began their study by identifying the different known sources of pollution coming from the Wankel, beginning with hydrocarbon. Hydrocarbons are a family of molecules, hexane, heptane, octane, and others, that consist of a chain of carbon atoms surrounded by hydrogen atoms. Essentially, they are fuels. In the case of exhaust from internal combustion engines, they are small portions of fuel that, for any of several reasons, may pass through the engine without being burned. A large portion of the unburned hydrocarbon output on any internal combustion engine is "wall quenching." Wall quenching occurs when the flame front reaches a relatively cool outer wall of the combustion chamber where it is extinguished a small distance from the wall, leaving in the remaining space raw fuel-air mixture, partially burned fuel, carbon monoxide, and other combustion byproducts. Most of these products go out with the exhaust; some remain to be burned on the next cycle.

Wall quenching accounts for a large amount of the HC produced by the Wankel, mostly because of the high surface to volume ratio of a Wankel engine. For a given engine displacement, there is a large amount of internal surface area where quench can occur. In a conventional piston engine, the charge only comes in contact with the surface of its individual cylinder. But in a rotary, the burning charge must move with the rotor, around the inside of the trochoidal housing, passing ever larger cool sidewall surfaces on its way to the exhaust port, quenching as it goes. The trailing apex seal then sweeps the unburned fuel that sticks to the trochoidal housing, and sends it out the exhaust.

Another portion of HC emission is accounted for by the "crevice effect," where two surfaces come so close to each other that the flame cannot propagate. If there is unburned fuel mixture in this region, it will also be swept into the exhaust, raising the HC levels. In the Wankel this occurs at the tips of the rotor when they approach the minor axis, and in the space between the rotor and the side housings above the side seals.

Combustion blowby is also a significant source of hydrocarbon emissions. In a piston engine, unburned mixture may leak past the rings to the crankcase where it could find its way to the atmosphere through the vent. Beginning in 1968, open crankcase vents were outlawed and manufacturers turned the vent inward, piping the gases from the crankcase back into the intake manifold where they could be reburned by the engine. A small amount of unburned fuel can also leak past the closed exhaust valve where it raises the exhaust hydrocarbon content. In a Wankel that uses side intake ports, any combustion leaking past the side seals will be vented back to the intake as the rotor sweeps past the intake ports, where it can mix with the incoming charge and be reburned. Some blowby leakage however, takes place past the leading apex seal where it goes out with the exhaust. In an engine with peripheral ports, more of the leakage past the side seals will find its way back into the exhaust.

Incomplete combustion is another large source of HC in gasoline engines is but a lesser factor with the Wankel. Thanks to the high turbulence inside the Wankel, the fuel mixture can be well distributed in the combustion chamber, and a Wankel runs well on the lean mixtures needed to minimize HC production from this source.

Carbon monoxide is usually produced under the same conditions as high HC, namely poor combustion. Any means employed to reduce HC emissions due to incomplete combustion will generally reduce CO emissions as well. Lean fuel/air ratios are particularly effective.

Nitrogen oxide is produced under the very high temperatures common in high compression engines. For conventional engine builders, NOx is usually the most difficult pollutant to control. It can be reduced by running a richer fuel mixture, but that of course increases HC and CO emissions. The Wankel rotary has a relatively cool peak combustion temperature compared to a piston engine, so NOx was not considered to be a problem for the Wankel.

In spite of the low peak combustion temperatures in a Wankel, the exhaust temperature at the port is several hundred degrees higher than in a conventional engine. The twin exhaust ports on a two rotor engine like the one in the study must each carry the exhaust of one half of the displacement of the engine instead of the one-sixth or one-eighth carried by a single port in a convention six or eight cylinder engine. Additionally, there is no cool-down time at the port, as the engine is continuously exhausting through it. Because of this, experiments at the University of Michigan would focus on the use of a thermal reactor and air injection to clean up the exhaust after it left the engine.

A thermal reactor today represents the most fundamental emission control device. As used on an automobile engine it is basically a heat stove, a baffled and insulated exhaust manifold. The baffles are designed to extend the path of the exhaust so that it spends more time in the reactor. The insulation keeps the exhaust temperature up. Simply put, the idea is to keep the fire going after it has left the engine and until all available fuel (HC) is burned up. In most designs, extra air is pumped in at the engine exhaust port to maintain the reaction.

Tests done at the University of Michigan were performed on an RC2-60U5 engine mounted in a dynamometer. Hydrocarbon readings were taken on an uncontrolled engine, an engine with a thermal reactor, and an engine with a thermal reactor and air injection. For the second part of the test, Curtiss-Wright installed an engine in a 1964 Ford Galaxy 500 sedan.

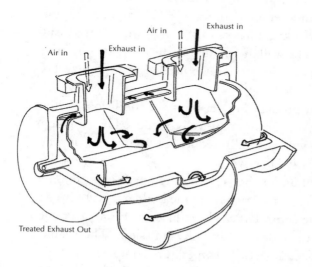

Figure 55. Thermal reactor used by Curtiss-Wright.

When an automobile is tested according to the EPA's federal test procedure, exhaust sampling begins from the time the car is started up cold. It is then sampled continuously while the car is taken through a series of accelerations and decelerations for about 40 minutes in an effort to simulate a drive through city traffic. The car is then stopped for 10 minutes, re-started, then driven through a short cycle about 10 minutes long to simulate stopping at a destination, parking the car for a short time, then driving away. The exhaust concentration is averaged over the distance driven and expressed as GPM (grams per mile).

Because the results are averaged over the duration of the test, an engine can fail the entire test because of a poor cold start. All gasoline engines are dirtier at cold start because of enriched fuel mixtures, larger degrees of wall quenching, incomplete combustion due to poor fuel mixture distribution, and cold exhaust. In many cases, the biggest challenge for manufacturers was getting their engines to clean up as quickly after cold start as possible.

The Wankel's high exhaust temperature proved to be its saving grace on cold starts. Thermal reactor systems (and catalytic converters that would later be employed) must come up to temperature before they can function, and at 1400 to 1600 degrees, the Wankel's exhaust brings them up to temperature quickly. Cold start results are improved, and the rest of the test is a breeze. Tests done by Cole and Jones were successful in significantly reducing the HC and CO output of the Wankel with the reactor and an air pump, and emissions were reduced further still by optimizing the fuel mixture, engine temperature and ignition timing.

Initial tests of the RC2-60 engine without benefit of emission controls showed that it produced more HC and CO than a comparable piston engine; the test engine, for instance, at 2000 rpm had in its exhaust around 400 to 500 parts per million HC. Under similar conditions with a thermal reactor, the HC output was reduced nearly 90 percent to about 75 parts per million. The engines were checked under a wide variety of conditions, and results consistently showed that the Curtiss-Wright Wankel engine could be brought into compliance with current laws with the installation of the thermal reactor and air pump.

After these thrilling test results, Cole and Jones were disappointed to find Curtiss-Wright seemed satisfied that it had done enough research on Wankel emissions. They stated in their 1970 paper for the SAE, "The extremely encouraging results from the RC engine with an exhaust reactor has had the indirect effect of thwarting further Curtiss-Wright fundamental engine research on this phase of the program. However, emission studies, both internal and external to the power section are being actively pursued at other NSU-Wankel licensees."

At the same time, Mazda was working with a thermal reactor and air pump system on its 10A engine. Mazda engineers had also achieved good results with optimizing sparkplug placement and, as they were using a twin sparkplug system, shutting down the trailing ignition during certain operating conditions. Test results were so good in fact that in the spring of 1972,

MAZDA emission control

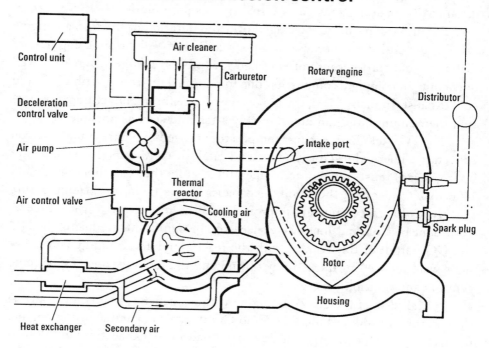

Figure 56. Mazda's emissions control system, mid–1970s.

about the same time Henry Ford was going on about the U.S. auto industry shutting down, Mazda caught the industry off guard by announcing rather matter of factly that it would have no trouble meeting 1975 U.S. emission standards.

While the Wankel's compact size had always been listed among its virtues, it was now looking that much better because it left more room under the hood for emission control equipment. Thermal reactors and air pumps are fairly large, and in an intermediate sized car with a V-8 engine, getting two thermal reactors and an air pump under the hood with the engine could require putting some very hot components in tight locations. A Wankel engine with its reactor and air pump system still took up less space than a conventional engine of similar output without emission controls.

Upcoming technology only made the Wankel look even better. Newer methods of cleaning up exhaust gas involved using catalytic converters, which passed the exhaust through a fine honeycombed ceramic that had been sprayed with platinum or rhodium. The platinum and rhodium act as a catalyzing agent to produce a chemical reaction that causes the carbon monoxide and the hydrocarbons to combine with free oxygen pumped into the exhaust by the air pump, converting them into carbon dioxide and water. It was a device that worked well on any engine, and worked very well downstream of a thermal reactor, but had one drawback: It could not tolerate any lead in the exhaust. Lead would quickly deposit on the catalyst and render it useless.

Oil companies had been putting tetraethyl lead in gasoline for years to produce the high octane gasoline needed by high compression engines. Lead was also considered to be important for lubricating the valves in their guides and where the valve face met the seat. The Wankel had already demonstrated that it did not need high-octane gasoline, and it had no valves to suffer from a lack of lead in the exhaust. So conversion to lead free fuel to preserve the catalytic converter would not be a problem for a Wankel powered car.

With these facts in mind, the major car manufacturers in the United States had to take another good hard look at the Wankel. Ford, General Motors, Chrysler, and International had all publicly admitted that they were having trouble cleaning up their engines. In late 1970, General Motors would announce that it had bought a license to produce Wankels and was beginning a development program of its own. As of the spring of 1972, only Mazda, with its RX-2 sedans, could say with confidence that they would be ready for the 1975 emission standards. The big American companies were getting worried, and the Wankel rotary was starting to look like salvation.

12

American Manufacturers
and the Wankel

General Motors had seemed to watch the Wankel story unfold during the 1960s with a kind of amused tolerance. New developments might raise an individual eyebrow, but as a company they had been unwilling to admit that the rotary would ever do anything more than fill a curious little market niche. Small companies like NSU might be able to market a few thousand cars a year, but the Wankel certainly had no future in the way GM built cars. But in November of 1970, GM publicly reversed its opinion of the Wankel and signed an agreement with Wankel GMBH for rights to produce engines in any size, shape and number. They paid dearly for coming into the game so late: $50 million was the figure quoted, to be paid in installments of $5 million each year. But then, General Motors never did anything in a small way.

In January of 1970, David Cole and Charles Jones presented to the Society of Automotive Engineers their paper describing their successful emissions research on the Curtiss-Wright RC2-60 engine. At the same meeting, Kenichi Yamamoto and Takashi Kuroda also presented a paper describing their intense rotary development program of the last ten years, problems they encountered, and how they had solved them. By the end of the meeting it was clear that many of the old concerns about the Wankel engine were either no longer considered a problem or would be manageable with further research. Curtiss-

Wright and Mazda's experience showed that the Wankel had come a long way in a very short time, and people in the know were optimistic about the engine's future. Those people included Ed Cole, president of General Motors.

Ed Cole had been with General Motors since the 1930s as an engineer. Like Roy Hurley of Curtiss-Wright, he liked to be considered an innovator and was open to new ideas about automotive propulsion. Cole was largely responsible for the Corvair, the most innovative (and ill-fated) car ever to come out of General Motors.

The Corvair was a compact, with a rectangular, bathtub-like shape that was becoming popular in European cars at the time. It had unit-body construction, four wheel independent suspension, and an air cooled, horizontally opposed, six cylinder engine mounted behind the rear axle line. While the car was initially successful, it soon became controversial because of some rather unusual handling characteristics. Between the weight of the car being heavily biased toward the rear, and the rear suspension being of the "swing axle" variety, which has a tendency to tuck the wheels under the car when heavily loaded in a turn, among people who knew their cars, the Corvair was considered unstable. The last straw fell when a young lawyer named Ralph Nader launched his career as a "consumer advocate" by publishing a book about the automotive industry called *Unsafe at Any Speed*, in which he used Cole's Corvair as an example of everything that was wrong with the automotive industry. In spite of the numerous re-designs that were intended to work out the car's bugs, Nader's book did irreparable damage to the Corvair's image and production tapered off until it stopped in 1969.

General Motors might have gone on to become quite a different type of company, one that would embrace innovation and lead the world in the development of new technologies. But thanks to the crash of the Corvair, many of the executives at GM were suspicious of new ideas, and quickly stifled any proposals that went too far out of well-charted territory. Much to their chagrin, however, Cole had been courting the Wankel for some time, and he rose through the corporate ranks while the engine was being developed.

An engineer who had worked for Curtiss-Wright during the early part of their Wankel program had a brother who worked at GM, Zora Duntov. Duntov had been designing Corvettes for Chevrolet for several years and had easy access to Cole. Receptive as always to the new technology, Cole wrote to NSU asking for an engine to study. NSU execs were a little confused about what to do, first because they didn't want to appear to be trying to make an end run around their agreement with Curtiss-Wright, and second because they were having endless problems with their apex seals. So Cole arranged to have a Prinz test car smuggled in via GM's subsidiaries, Opel in Germany and Vauxhall in Britain. Meanwhile, Curtiss-Wright supplied one of their engines to study.[1]

As the years went by, GM's interest in the Wankel waxed and waned according to who was in control at the time. Cole was an ardent supporter of the new engine, but opinions varied throughout the company. When the threat of government emission regulations became more and more real, Curtiss-Wright engaged Ed Cole's son, David, who was a professor of automotive engineering at the University of Michigan, to do some research work on emissions reduction. The results of the research were published about the time that the automakers were starting to groan about how strict the new emissions regulations were. Ed Cole was president now and still saw the Wankel engine as a big part of the company's future.

So GM got a piece of the Wankel, under an agreement that was unique compared to other companies. While other companies were sharing information, GM was not obligated to share any new developments or technology. Of course, that also meant that GM was not entitled to information on other companies' developments. There were no restrictions on the size or output of the engines that GM could build, and the payments were to come in $5 million installments with the option to terminate at any time. There were no per-unit royalty payments. The agreement spanned the five years from 1971 to 1976.

The automotive world seemed to have been waiting for one of the major U.S. manufacturers to commit to rotary production. All of the major companies had closet Wankel advocates in their administrative departments just waiting for a sign that the time was right to come out in favor of the Wankel. Once the General Motors deal was announced, everyone expected to hear from Ford, Chrysler and American Motors to see what their plans would be. Toyo Kogyo was happy for the competition. C.R. Brown, their general manager in California, said that it made it look like Toyo Kogyo had known what they were doing when they started building Wankels. Ford tried in 1971 to get a piece of the action by negotiating to buy 20 percent of Toyo Kogyo, but as the company's U.S. sales took off, negotiations became "very difficult," as quoted with typical Japanese understatement.[2] In the end, Ford was offered 20 percent of everything *except* the rotary project—in other words, 20 percent of nothing. A spokesman for Ford stated, "The Japanese really left us standing at the altar."[3] In hopes of staying in the game, Ford began shopping for 15,000–20,000 rotary engines to offer as options in 1975 or 1976 models of the Capri, Maverick, or a restyled Mustang on a Pinto frame. But they were not finding any bargains. Comotor was asking about twice the price of a comparable piston engine, and Toyo Kogyo was unwilling to sell at all until 1975. Ford's other option was to manufacture and import engines from its European arm Fordwerke A.G. of West Germany, which held a three-year license to make rotaries, but importing them would put Ford in the position of having to pay royalties to Curtiss-Wright.

Despite the obstacles, auto industry analysts felt sure that Ford would come around and announce its own rotary program at any time. But Henry Ford II said in a September 1972 press conference, "We are not negotiating, and we don't plan to." This did not stop observers from speculating, though, as they had heard the public denial and private maneuvering routine before.

Ford had shown some interest in acquiring a license agreement in the early days, but representatives were not very impressed with what they saw when they visited Neckarsulm in 1961. They were more interested in buying a finished product than an engine that was still in need of years of intense development.

At Chrysler, Alan Loofbourrow, vice president for engineering and research, expressed public contempt for the Wankel, saying, "It will turn out to be one of the most unbelievable fantasies ever to hit the world auto industry."[4] Chrysler looked at the Wankel in the early sixties and deemed it too "smokey." They didn't see any promise in the early engines and chose instead to bet on turbine engines for an alternative power source, a bet that lost. Loofbourrow plainly stated that Chrysler had no intention of introducing a rotary car, but if General Motors did first, they probably would have one in the next model year. He acknowledged that Chrysler was shopping for rotary engines to meet that contingency.

American Motors president William Luneburg said that nothing dramatic would happen with rotaries through 1980, but down the hall, Gerald Meyers, his vice president for products, said that American Motors could convert 50 percent to rotaries by 1980 and 100 percent by 1984. American Motors was negotiating for a production license, and Meyers suggested that they would probably be buying engines from Curtiss-Wright while they were developing their own, intending to introduce them in the Gremlin X models.[5]

The financial world, as usual, was running on rumors. In May of 1971 the *Wall Street Journal* ran a feature article by Richard Martin that suggested that the best way to get a company's stock to move up was to (1) rename the company "The Wankel Works"; (2) announce the receipt of a contract to make a screw that might be used in Wankel engines; (3) announce the hiring of three scientists to look into Wankel engine research; and (4) announce that a clerk in the shipping room has a brother-in-law who is thinking about buying a car that has a Wankel engine. All kidding aside, stocks were indeed going wild wherever the Wankel was mentioned in what was otherwise a fairly dismal market. Curtiss-Wright's stock went up by more than 400 percent in the first half of 1972 on the strength of their royalty assets. With their comprehensive rights that they had negotiated in 1959, they were in a position to get a piece of every Wankel engine built or sold in the United States except for those built under General Motors' license. Investors looked anywhere they could for an opportunity to get in on the Wankel for a bargain. Machine tool companies were doing well, particularly Babcock & Wilcox and Gleason Works which were designing tools for grinding trochoids and other parts appropriate for Wankel engines. Every time General Motors made a real-estate purchase there was speculation that it was for their new Wankel production facility.

The only place where General Motors' dabbling with the Wankel got more interest was in the motoring press. They were eager to report any hint of news on the Wankel, particularly General Motors' version, that they could get. At first General Motors was fairly reticent. But after a closed meeting of 700 GM officers in a secluded location in November of 1972, one group executive, John Z. DeLorean, was quoted as saying, "At least one proposed program shows rotary engines in 80 to 100 percent of our automobiles within the next ten years."[6] Of course a remark like that could get everyone excited.

General Motors began a crash program of rotary engine development with the optimistic target of introduction in 1973 as an extra cost option in the Vega. It was called GMRCE for General Motors Rotary Combustion Engine. Soon the proposed introduction date was moved back to summer of 1974. Prototypes were built, but the performance was not really inspiring. Even though the rotary Vega had more horsepower than the standard Vega, the extra weight associated with the rotary engine was enough to even out the balance (remember the NSU Sport Prinz), and the two cars had very similar performance.

General Motors played its cards fairly close to the chest during the rotary development program. The company released few details about its original rotary engine while engineers were working on it, but it was clear that it was a departure from those made by the rest of the world. The engine GM began researching was made entirely of nodular cast iron. Ignition was by single spark plugs. The inner trochoidal housing was not plated, but was sprayed with a metallic coating. The apex seals were made of a ceramic material. During early development, the engineers wanted to design for a quick and simple apex seal replacement as in the NSU engine so the life expectancy of the apex seals could be comparatively short. But the GM engineers' first concepts did not last long, and like most new Wankel licensees, they ran into trouble with their design and took a good hard look at the Mazda engines to solve some of their problems. They changed the rotor housings to aluminum, like everyone else in the rotary business, citing improved heat dissipation properties. But while Mazda used a sprayed chrome surface on the inside of their housings, General Motors preferred to lift a little of the technology they gained with the Chevrolet Vega, an early attempt at building piston engines with cylinder walls made of an aluminum silicone alloy instead of steel. This made the housing surface more similar to the Nickasil coating used by NSU and Comotor than they were to Mazda. At one point, engineers said that the GM Wankel could even come with aluminum end plates, where other manufacturers were using steel. Once again the final design steered more toward Mazda practice and used aluminum housings with chrome plating and end covers of cast iron. General Motors hoped to be able to eliminate the external oil cooler that was present on nearly every other production Wankel, citing decreased manufacturing cost and increased reliability. Other companies were skeptical about their chances. The oil-cooled rotor was central to most successful Wankel rotary designs and a means for controlling oil temperature should not be discarded lightly.

The third generation GM rotary would have twin ignition systems like the Mazda, fired by high energy transistorized ignition systems, mostly to minimize exhaust emissions rather than for improved performance. GM wanted to install their rotary without what they called Mazda's "albatross," referring to the 20 pound thermal reactor that Mazda used to bring the Wankel into compliance with U.S. emission control standards. To do this, they would have to clean up the engine's combustion. Toward this end the GMRCE was equipped with a new carburetor built by Rochester Products dubbed "Integrated Fuel Control." The new carburetor used variable venturis, engine vacuum and altitude compensation to control fuel distribution more precisely. It appealed as an inexpensive compromise between conventional carburetors and the electronic fuel injection systems that were showing up on European cars.[7]

Probably the most anticipated rotary car from General Motors would be a Wankel-powered Corvette. In June 1970, *Motor Trend* magazine announced that GM was drawing up plans for a mid-engined Corvette. Ferrari, Maserati, Lamborghini, and other famous sports car makers were all building mid-engined cars at the time, so it only seemed to make sense for General Motors' flagship sportscar. In December 1971, *Motor Trend* announced that the mid-engined 'Vette would be Wankel powered.

Not long after General Motors acquired a license to build Wankels, GM vice president Bill Mitchell had the design staff begin working on a concept Corvette suitable for display, using a GM rotary engine. Mitchell was approaching retirement age, and having been designing Corvettes since the 1961 model year, he would have liked very much to complete his career with a completely new and radical Corvette to place among his designing trophies. Mitchell gave the project to Clare MacKichan and his design staff but monitored it closely. The designers played with a number of concepts including front-wheel drive, but came back to the mid-engined, rear drive car, with engine and transaxle mounted transversely. There was a consensus among the designers that the Corvette had gotten too big and heavy, so they wanted to aim for a smaller car, one about the size of the Ferrari Dino.

The first full sized model was completed in June of 1971. As a step in the design process, it was a complete model showing the interior and placement of machinery as well as the shape of the exterior. The model was shown to the management accompanied by a detailed report on the engineering and production of the car. The bosses were pleased with what they were shown and approved the construction of a running prototype.

The GMRCE was coupled with a new automatic transaxle that existed thanks to project XP-987, a program to develop a front wheel drive car in the Nova class. The engine was offset about seven inches to the right of the car centerline, which left room for the transmission on the left. Plans included developing a four-speed manual for production cars. The engine used in the prototype was straight off the shelf at R&D and used a single Rochester Quadra-jet carburetor rather than the new IFC model. The engine, a 266 cubic inch two-rotor, was not equipped for emissions control at all and produced 180 horsepower at 6100 rpm with much potential for further development. The research and development staff had not quite been able to eliminate the oil cooler, but they hid it in the coolant surge tank in the form of a liquid-liquid heat exchanger.

Initially, to save costs, engineers were tempted to use front end components from the Vega, but they later settled on McPherson struts with longitudinal torsion bars, similar to the system used by Porsche. Rear suspension was done by trailing arms with coil-over shock assemblies.

The prototype 'Vette went from the model stage to a running show car in less than a year. The remarkable speed of the project reflected the commitment of the company and the people involved. They wanted the Wankel

Corvette to become a reality. The styling had a very European look which was a real departure for the Corvette and for American car companies of the 1970s. It would shock the Corvette traditionalists, but it showed the class in which GM hoped to compete—a class dominated by the Italian exotics or even the Mercedes C111, if that ever got past prototype stage.

The only prospect at General Motors more exciting than the Wankel Corvette idea was the four rotor Corvette concept. The four rotor prototype was built on a chassis that GM had used to display a new mid-engine experimental Corvette with a transversely mounted V-8. The sideways mounted engine was connected to an Olds Toronado type automatic transmission, which was also mounted transversely and passed the power below and in front of the engine. At the transmission's output end, a set of spiral bevel gears sent the power down a fore-aft mounted shaft that passed back through the sump of the engine and connected to a differential just beneath and behind the engine. It seemed a Rube Goldberg kind of design, but it enabled the engineers to use a lot of off-the-shelf parts.

It was a similar inspiration that brought about the four rotor Corvette. GM had earlier decided that they did not want to build any rotary engines with more than two rotors because they didn't want to have to cope with the design problems associated with supporting the shaft in the center and assembling a gear into it. It was a problem that could be handled, as Curtiss-Wright had shown, but it required some expensive, close-tolerance machining. Chevrolet engineers wanted a four-rotor engine, so they installed two of the GMRCE engines in tandem, replacing the V-8 with a more powerful and relatively compact four-rotor package.[8]

The two engines were joined via a welded steel box made of quarter inch plate. The eccentric shafts were joined by a splined sleeve with the planes of the eccentrics of the two engines placed 90 degrees out of phase to maintain even firing impulses. The sleeve had a sprocket attached for a toothed belt. The belt drove a distributor above the engine, an alternator, and at the bottom of the engine the engine oil pump. The right engine had the oil sump; the left engine had only a shallow pan that drained into the right. Each engine had its own Quadra-jet carburetor; again the four rotor Corvette was built without attempting to comply with emissions regulations, so horsepower figures were only spoken in terms of potential. But as the GMRCE engines were known to easily produce 150 horsepower, estimates for the four rotor Corvette put it over 300.

The design staff and the motoring press eagerly anticipated the approval of the new Corvette designs, but it was not to be. The two rotor 'Vette prototype was shown to the GM board of directors during an annual new products display. Richard Gerstenberg, chairman of the board, said, "What do you want a new Corvette for? You're selling all the cars you can make right now!" It was hard to argue the point—after all, it was business.

Ed Cole and Bill Mitchell wanted the new Corvettes to happen, and they were supported by a lot of good press that the prototypes received. It might have been a good time for a change, and having had a record profit year in 1973, General Motors could afford to take the chance, but very shortly the Wankel engine was to fall out of favor with the world and General Motors would suspend all of their Wankel operations indefinitely.

13

Mazda Comes
to America

While GM was taking a crash course in rotary engine technology, Mazda was pinning its hopes on selling its rotary-engine cars to Americans. The company was heavily in debt, and president Tsuneji Matsuda had rejected overtures from financiers who could have reduced the company's debt in exchange for a piece of the rotary action. Rather, he chose to take his chances with the American market. But marketing automobiles in the 1970s was hardly the science that it would later become, with teaser advertising campaigns and carefully timed releases of products and information. Mazda had a few small dealerships in the United States, one in Seattle, one in Miami, one in Houston, and a headquarters in Los Angeles with plenty of empty space in between. Mazda went looking for a manager to bring some order to their sketchy American network.

It was C.R. "Dick" Brown who was given credit for Mazda's marketing success during this time. A veteran of Chrysler and American Motors, Brown was appointed to the position of general manager in the United States in December of 1970, and saw his appointment as the opportunity of a lifetime.[1] When he joined Mazda of America, the organization consisted of five Japanese employees, one bilingual temporary secretary, and a few rented desks and typewriters in a warehouse in Los Angeles.

Mazdas were already selling themselves on their own quirky virtues when Brown took control, but he recognized the need for a national campaign to enlighten the rest of the public about Mazda automobiles and their revolutionary rotary engine. (Mazda did not call their engine a Wankel, claiming that they had spent enough time and money developing it that they could call it anything they wanted.) Brown set to work organizing such an effort.

America was good to Mazda at first. While in 1970 Mazda sold only 2000 cars, in 1971 they sold 21,000 and in 1972 60,000. Those figures were relatively small, especially by Detroit standards, but they made Mazda the fifth largest selling import in America, ahead of Fiat, Volvo, Capri, and 17 other importers. All this was accomplished without benefit of automatic transmissions or national advertising, and through a very sketchy (but growing) dealer network. In December of 1972, Mazda opened 80 new dealerships from Chicago to New York, screening 2300 applications for the 80 openings. Even though the ante for opening a Mazda dealership was $650,000, there was no shortage of applicants. Mazda's average dealer was selling 49 cars a month, grossing $606 per car ($225 more than the industry average).

Word had already spread among the auto enthusiasts. Many people had been following the Wankel engine for years in automotive journals and were waiting for a dealership to come to or even near their town so they could line up to buy a Mazda.

Reviews from owners were good. The RX-2, aside from having the unique engine that the buyers were looking for, was said to be an excellent car. The fit and finish was good, and automotive journalists praised the way the controls were placed, saying everything fell easily to hand and worked well. But it was the performance that was most surprising.

"The power comes on easily," reported *Motor Trend*. "It's not like one of those engines that have to be nursed along like a sick mule unless you're driving flat out. It starts easily and runs quietly, and you can tool lazily around all day never turning it more than 4000 rpm, just like any other mild-mannered piece of family transportation. But when you need the fire of Zeus, you just put your foot in all the way, hold it there to its 6500 rpm redline, and you can suck the doors off of anything not specifically built for setting drag strips on fire."[2]

Such superlative reviews were not uncommon, mostly because the RX-2 looked like so many other economy imports but ran like a Toyota with a V-8 under the hood. People just weren't used to that kind of power coming from a Japanese import.

As word of the RX-2's many virtues was spreading, Brown hired Bill

Power, a man with whom he had worked at Chrysler, to be advertising and sales promotion manager. Power, along with the advertising agency Foote, Cone and Belding, created the advertisements that made the Mazda rotary engine just as famous among the non-automotive public as it was among the motorheads.

Power and the agency knew that they needed to create advertisements that would illustrate just what was so different about their engine to a public that knew or cared little about what made an automobile engine work to begin with. Someone in the agency came up with a radio commercial that told their audience that, while a piston engine went "boing-boing-boing," a Mazda rotary "goes 'Hmmmmmm.'" It was a great little jingle that was memorable and translated well into television, accompanied by the image of a kid on a pogo stick, Not only did it made the Mazda name familiar, but it passed the greatest test of success: it was parodied by famous musicians. Such an honor is probably as close as commercials get to a hall of fame.

As sales in the states continued to climb, Matsuda and Brown became euphoric. They openly predicted selling 300,000 cars in America in 1975 and speculated about taking the place of American Motors as the number four automobile company in the country.[3] Statistics showed that aside from cutting into the market of other Japanese imports, they were cutting into the sales of European sports cars like BMW and Alfa Romeo. Even Ford was losing Mustang customers to the hot little sedan. But even as business seemed to be taking off, problems were reaching the surface. Reports of engines that were failing prematurely and of poor gas mileage, always one of the rotary's weaker areas, were about to become a major issue.

In 1973 J.D. Power, a market research firm known for its objectivity, published the results of polls conducted with Mazda owners. The surveys covered R100 owners as well as RX-2 owners. It revealed that for the most part, the owners they interviewed were happy with their cars and would recommend them to a friend, but it was turning out to be a high maintenance machine, which made some people nervous. Spark plug life was short and oil consumption was high (about 1000 miles to a quart), making it necessary for the owner to pay more attention to what was under the hood than the average American driver cared to. Owners also said it was difficult to find qualified service technicians outside of the dealer network and sometimes it was hard inside as well. So small problems might often be exacerbated by bad service.

In the R100 engine, the group found a pattern failure with an oil seal. It wasn't the notorious apex seal but the round oil seal that prevented the cooling oil in the rotor from moving up into the space between the rotor and the side housings. It was made of a rubber O ring and after about 30,000 miles was subject to failure, causing exhaust smoke and excessive oil consumption. Mazda reacted by changing the ring material to Teflon and offering to replace them for free.

Consumer Reports, which had bought a 1971 RX-2 for evaluation, reported a different failure at 25,000 miles. The O ring seals between the iron side housings and the aluminum trochoid housings failed, allowing coolant to leak into the combustion chambers, which caused a loss of power and difficulty in starting. Mazda redesigned the seals, adding a metal strip to protect the seals from the heat of the combustion side of the engine, and extended the engine warranty to 50,000 miles. They fixed the engine for *Consumer Reports*, but the magazine reported having been contacted by owners describing numerous bad scenarios when they tried to get their rotaries fixed under warranty. In the end the magazine advised readers not to buy an RX-2 made before August of 1972 unless they could obtain documentation that the car in question had already had the redesigned seals installed.

Surveys by Power and *Consumer Reports* also brought up the gas mileage issue. Owners reported that the cars were relatively thirsty, averaging only about 17.3 miles per gallon in urban driving. Enthusiasts justified it by pointing out that the mileage wasn't bad for a performance car, which is what they considered their Mazdas to be, but the average buyer who looked for economy in a Japanese import was disappointed.

There were many ironies in the story of the rotary's development, but the largest one was the relationship of Mazda with the EPA. Earlier, in 1972, it was Mazda's announcement that its rotary engine would meet the EPA standards for 1975 that attracted the attention of the entire automotive industry. In 1973, it would be the very test procedures that the EPA used that would eventually scuttle Mazda's sales in America.

The EPA tested the cars on a chassis dynamometer, or "rolling road" as the British call it. Exhaust gases were sampled from cold start-up, through a short warm-up and a series of accelerations and decelerations designed to simulate driving through a large city like downtown Los Angeles. After the samples were analyzed and the levels of pollutants were measured, the EPA used CO_2 concentrations to calculate theoretical gas mileage. Under these conditions, the RX-2's performance was dismal, results showing theoretical gas mileage of just over 10 miles per gallon in city driving.

While everyone at Mazda had to admit that gas mileage was not the rotary's best area, nobody was willing to accept the EPA's figures. Mazda published its own figures, and certain motoring magazines conducted independent tests verifying that under ideal conditions, an RX-2 could get as much as 20 mpg. Brown did his best to control the damage, protesting that the EPA's conditions were far from ideal. It was true, they weren't, but they were indeed objective. All car models to be sold in the United States were run through the same battery of tests; unfortunately it seemed that these tests had accidentally zeroed in on all the least efficient modes of operation for the RX-2. The EPA responded by saying that, while the gas mileage figures might not be accurate for actual driving conditions, the relative figures from car to car would be accurate, and it was true that the Mazdas used considerably more fuel than their imported brethren.

Brown insisted that the EPA test the RX-2 on a more typical driving cycle, and results showed that the RX-2 was indeed capable of 20 mpg, but when competing cars were tested on the same driving cycle, they all performed better. The damage was done, and the Mazda rotary had become infamous as a gas guzzler.

In the grand scheme of things, it could not have happened at a worse time. Later in the year (October to be more specific), war would break out between forces of Egypt and Syria, and forces of Israel. Such a thing would seem unrelated to the fortunes of a small Japanese car company in the United States, but it nearly finished off any chance that Mazda had to sell cars in America.

Because the United States supported Israel in the conflict, and Egypt was supported by its Arab neighbors, the members of OPEC (Organization of Petroleum Exporting Countries) united to stop exporting oil to America. With crude oil supplies drastically cut, the price of oil products, especially gasoline, rose sharply. Oil companies cut production and distribution, reporting that crude was in short supply. Whether that was in fact true was the subject of much speculation, but the point was moot for Mazda. Long lines formed at filling stations, lines filled with people who were promising themselves as they waited that if they ever got out of there, they were going to buy a car that would go farther on a gallon of gas.

In 1973, Mazda's sales peaked at 119,000. In January of 1974, sales fell off by over 50 percent from the year before. Sales continued to drop off, and unsold cars were accumulating at the ports and the factory. By the end of 1974, Toyo Kogyo had 210,000 unsold cars in inventory, 160,000 in Japan and 50,000 in the United States.

As Toyo Kogyo's fortunes in America became more tenuous, the bankers had to move in. The Sumitomo bank was holding over a billion dollars of paper from the company and was desperate to keep it alive. Toyo Kogyo employed around 36,000 people in the Hiroshima area, and to allow the company to shut down would have wrecked the economy of southern Japan.[4]

Engineer Yamamoto said that he was sure that he could improve gas mileage by 40 percent if given the time and money. He was exploring stratified charge systems, a field that Curtiss-Wright was already heavily into. Stratifying the charge meant that the incoming fuel air/mixture would form into layers of different density in the combustion chamber. It could be achieved in the Wankel with careful design of the intake tract and the shape of the cut-out in the rotor. A large portion of the charge would be of a mixture strength that would normally be too lean to be useful, but by lighting the richer layer, the lean layer could be ignited and burned also. This process generally yielded higher gas mileage and lower emissions.

The bankers continued to finance Yamamoto's research efforts while they struggled to keep the company alive in the United States. Mazda was still producing and selling conventional cars and a line of small pickup trucks including, for a short time, a rotary pickup truck. So they chose to shift the emphasis away from the rotary engines and push the piston cars while rotary research continued in the lab. Future marketing strategy would be to focus on the rotary's qualities as a high performance engine rather than a passenger car engine.

14

Who Owned the Wankel?

For years NSU had survived on the income from its Wankel licensees, but it seemed that the company could not produce a self-sustaining population of Wankel powered cars in any form. NSU Spiders had become famous for apex seal failures, reportedly because the engine had not seen enough testing in the stop-and-start driving conditions of the real world and when subjected to this kind of abuse, the apex seals became brittle and often cracked. When they did crack, their owners also had trouble finding qualified mechanics. So even the job of apex seal replacement, which was supposed to be a simple procedure, could not be performed correctly. Hoping to maintain a good image for their troublesome child, NSU initiated a policy of replacing engines for dissatisfied customers for free, which led to crippling repair costs for the company. NSU hoped to redeem the Wankel with their RO 80, but it turned out that it couldn't stand up to the real world any better than the Spider engines could.

The new twin rotor engine in the RO 80 also had not been tested well enough at slow speeds under the stop and start conditions of real driving, and on the road in the hands of owners the engines did not last. In a survey taken by *Auto, Motor und Sport* of 191 RO 80 owners who had driven an average of 20,000 miles since the cars were new, 25 percent of the cars had broken down on the highway at least once, 75 percent had starting trouble, and half had had rotor or bearing failures that required replacement of the engine. The car's frequent failures became a popular joke. When RO 80s passed each other on the highway, the drivers would hold up a number of fingers to indicate how many times the apex seals had been replaced since the car was new. The average number was three.[1] In spite of their problems though, NSU sold some 27,000 RO 80s.

But 27,000 cars was not enough to make a profit. The company had been in trouble for a while, and von Heydekampf was looking for a partner to help prop it up. An earlier proposed deal with Citroën had fallen apart, and he was now speaking with Kurt Lotz, who had been recently appointed as director of Volkswagen.

Volkswagen could have bought NSU outright, but instead it agreed to a merger between Audi and NSU. Volkswagen, being the owner of Audi, thereby gained a 60 percent stake in NSU. And because it was not a direct acquisition by Volkswagen, the deal could go through without the permission of Volkswagen's stockholders, including the federal and provincial governments. Volkswagen would not pay any cash to the shareholders of NSU, who might see their stock devalued as they became a smaller portion of a larger company.

In addition to acquiring the rotary, VW also stood to get a new car that had not yet been produced. NSU had on the drawing board the K-70, a mid-sized front wheel drive car that could be fitted with either a rotary or conventional engine. For Volkswagen, the K70 would have been direct competition for the 411, a mid-sized car driven by an air-cooled rear mounted engine. The 411 would be Volkswagen's first (though unsuccessful) attempt to move into an upscale market.

But the move did not go off smoothly. Von Heydekampf and Lotz announced that the merger was under way and, in an attempt to satisfy NSU stockholders who might be opposed to the merger, they claimed that the income from the Wankel engine would be a separate part of the business and that NSU shareholders would be issued *genusscheine*, or shares in the profits from the Wankel. The *genusscheine* were immediately traded in the stock market, but only as hypothetical paper because they had not actually been issued. The market was getting Wankel fever again and investors were behaving irrationally, seriously overvaluing the shares in hopes of cashing in on the coming rotary revolution. Even if they did exist, the *genusscheine* weren't worth what they had been trading for. Stock market officials eventually put a stop to their trading and when the details of the deal came out, NSU stockholders and people who had bought *genusscheine* were outraged.

Among the outraged was the Israeli British Bank, which had been buying NSU stock for years and by then had accumulated over 10 percent of the stock outright and had obtained the proxy support of another 15 percent. By German law, a vote of 25 percent is enough to block any move by the company. The bank sent Joshua Bension, one of their directors; Elihu Miron, an Israeli lawyer; and Lois Erdl, a German lawyer, to negotiate details of the merger with Volkswagen.

The group put forth their demands, promising to block the merger if they were not satisfied. They proposed increasing the value of the *genusscheine* by extending their life from 10 to 15 years and increasing NSU shareholders' stake in the Wankel profits from two-fifths to two-thirds. They wanted Volkswagen to pay royalties if it produced Wankel engined cars, they wanted NSU to be compensated for development costs on the K70 which NSU developed but VW intended to market, and they wanted assurance that the rights of the *genusscheine* could not be taken away.

At first VW did not believe that the bankers controlled as many votes as they claimed, so they decided to call their bluff, Miron and Bension quickly produced a batch of proxy votes from Erdl's office that represented more than 10 percent of the company and assured VW that more were coming. Volkswagen yielded and with the representatives of the IBB, they prepared for a stockholders' meeting. The meeting was attended by about 1000 shareholders including Wankel, who remained anonymous and unnoticed in the crowed, and the mood was one of suspicion. Minority shareholders felt that they were being had by the bankers and VW and they were not easily reassured.

Eventually, as a result of that meeting in 1969, NSU became Audi-NSU-Auto Union, but not right away. Accusations flew back and forth in the meeting, but one that seemed to stick was that Lotz was trying to buy up remaining NSU stock on the cheap and had made dealings during the merger that had never been made public. He had had a clause inserted in the merger contract that had the new company of Audi-NSU-Auto Union paying a substantial fee to Volkswagen to compensate Volkswagen for the organizational and tax advantages it had gained in the merger. The fee came from money that normally would have been paid out to stockholders as dividends. Lotz claimed that he had mailed the documents about the deal to von Heydekampf, but they had been lost in the mails.

But it was Lotz's insultingly low offer for the remainder of NSU stock that set the Israeli bankers off. Miron went to the court on behalf of the minority shareholders and was able to get injunctions suspending the takeover, so NSU remained independent for a time. It was not until 1971, after Lotz was replaced, that VW was able to negotiate a settlement with the bankers and purchase the remaining NSU stock for three times the price offered by Lotz.[2]

Wankel had formed his own company earlier, when he aligned himself with Ernst Hutzenlaub to form Wankel GmbH. Hutzenlaub had put up $250,000 of his own money for the development of the engine in its early days at NSU and received for his money 50 percent of the royalties taken in by the new company. In 1971, royalties for rotary engines built outside the US were split up with NSU getting 54 percent (which was distributed via Volkswagen to holders of the *genusscheine*), Wankel GmbH getting 36 percent, and Curtiss-Wright getting 10 percent. But on engines built within the United States, Curtiss-Wright got 60 percent, NSU, 24 percent and Wankel 16 percent.[3] Wankel and Hutzenlaub had also formed another company, Rotary Engines, a subsidiary of Wankel GmbH to pay for research done by third parties.

By 1969, Wankel and Hutzenlaub were ready to sell their companies and, with several people acting as agents, began entertaining bids. Max Bunford, who had tried to engineer the merger between NSU and Citroën, made an offer, as did the Israeli British Bank, who still held 14 pecent of NSU stock. General Motors became interested because purchasing the company would mean that they would not have to purchase a license to produce the engine, but they were spooked by threats of antitrust litigation should they wrap up rights to the engine and withdrew their offer. Eventually, the winning offer came from a company called Lonrho (London and Rhodesian Estates) in the person of Roland "Tiny" Rowland. But like many things touched by Rowland, the deal was shrouded in controversy. The IBB and Max Bunford were among the minor investors in the deal while Lonrho was to have bought 80 percent of Wankel. Rowland settled on a price of 100 million marks (about $25 million at the exchange rate) but the paperwork showed him paying 64 million marks at settlement with the balance being paid from the annual license payments that General Motors had now committed to. When this financial sleight of hand surfaced, Rowland was in big trouble with the board of directors of Lonrho as well as his investment partners.

The board of directors tried to dismiss Rowland, charging that he had misled them as to the true nature and cost of the deal he had made. Rowland's counter was to appeal to the stockholders in a special meeting, but he had go to the courts to keep the board from dismissing him before the special meeting.

A board member testified that Rowland had invited him to report to the full board on the nature of the deal for the Wankel companies and that he had done so, equipped only with the knowledge of what Rowland had told him. At that time, the board approved the deal under the impression that they were buying 100 percent of the companies for 64 million marks. But the next day, the board gave Rowland the authority to negotiate "in his absolute discretion," the authority he used to increase the price and lower the percentage.

Wilkinson further reported that the details of the deal were kept from him and that as they came out, Rowland further misled him about the liability of the further payments. Rowland claimed that all the details were spelled out in the papers he submitted to Wilkinson, but the papers were all in German, a language that Wilkinson did not use well. The issue of whether Rowland had misled the board and should be dismissed became moot when during the litigation, South African police arrested several of the senior executives of Lonrho including a member of the board of directors and charged them with fraud. Two more members of the board resigned and Rowland maintained control of the company, his opposition having been severely weakened by the scandal.

Negotiations continued, each side trying to extract every extra mark out of the other, some members playing both sides, one sitting on the board of Lonrho and trying to drive up the price of the deal for a kickback from Hutzenlaub. Rowland was eventually able to have the rest of his opposition removed from the board by wielding his popular support among the stockholders of Lonrho, and he pushed for completion of the buyout. In the end, Wankel and Hutzenlaub got their 64 million marks, plus the additional 36 million to be paid within two years. Lonrho also paid several liabilities of Wankel GmbH including a substantial pension for Wankel, and a large payment to Frau Hoeppner, the widow of Wankel's chief designer.

Rowland got what he wanted for his company's money, which was a piece of every Wankel engine made, a piece of every Wankel license sold, and a piece of the fees paid by companies who had bought a license but produced no Wankels. Wankel GmbH and Rotary Engines under the ownership of Lonrho became a vehicle for collecting revenue off of any rotary engine business taking place. As such, they were an excellent investment, but did not live up to Wankel's original intention of being a center of research and development for rotary engines.

It was Dankwert Eiermann who got Wankel GmbH back on track. He had worked with Wankel since 1961 and became chief engineer and chief executive while Wankel GmbH was still under control of Lonrho. In or around 1975, under the direction of Eiermann the company developed engines of all types, including aircraft engines, heavy fuel engines, and compressors—some for sale, most for research.

Eiermann was eventually able to find financial backing from Juergan Bax, an automotive industrialist, and with his help bought Wankel GmbH from Lonrho. He established a new headquarters in Korb, near Stuttgart, and closed the Lindau facility that had been the center of Wankel's operations. The new headquarters was dubbed the World Wankel Center by its owners. There they continue research and development on different principles and applications for Wankel technology. Their areas of study include not just automotive aircraft and marine engines, but also pumping technology such as superchargers, large air pumps for ventilation, and air conditioning compressors.

15

The Rotary Turnaround

With the fortunes of Mazda failing, other companies took another good hard look at their rotary programs and compared them to the successes or failures of others. NSU's record with rotary cars was followed by auto industry analysts right up to their buyout by VW-Audi. Audi was reportedly planning a rotary powered car but it backed out and instead installed a piston engine in the car intended for the rotary and sold it in the United States as the 100LS.

Mercedes had teased the world with their concept cars and talk about rotary powered sedans and diesel trucks, but they backed away from the rotary position, watching the developments as Mazda and NSU tried to market their new cars. The C111 which had been such an exciting car as a showcase for the Wankel had become a test mule, some examples having their Wankel engines removed and replaced by other engines that Mercedes was testing—even diesels. Friedrich Flick, who controlled Mercedes-Benz at the time, once told Roland Berner of Curtiss-Wright that Mercedes could not introduce a Wankel powered car because the worldwide scale on which they operated required them to use poorly skilled workers to provide service in less developed countries. They did not think it wise to introduce a radical new engine into their markets under these conditions because it could not be well serviced.

Everyone still seemed to be looking to General Motors to redeem the Wankel, but GM just wasn't coming through. With each passing model year, they put off the introduction of their new rotary engine Vega, until it became not a Vega at all, but a Vega sized car built for the rotary engine in 1975. Then in September of 1974, General Motors announced that they were postponing indefinitely the introduction of a rotary powered car. After watching GM push back the date for two years, many readers interpreted the word "postponing" correctly as "cancelling." The proposed Vega or Vega sized car was never marketed with the rotary.

General Motors was not candid about their reasons for giving up on the rotary. Their public position on the rotary in 1974 was that they were barely able to make the engine meet the emissions standards for 1975 and that they had little hope of bringing it into line with the ever tightening standards of 1977.

With that kind of outlook, it made little sense for the company to introduce a new engine that only had a useful production life of two years. No doubt, they were also considering Mazda's trials with the EPA and consumer groups who had branded their car a "gas guzzler" in a time when such a label could have a huge effect on sales.

But industry analysts and automotive journalists were not accepting that as the whole story. Just before Ed Cole retired from General Motors in 1974, he said in a news release, "Whatever you've seen or heard about the reason the GM rotary was delayed, it's not the real reason."

GM had always been very tight lipped about their rotary program. Their license to produce Wankel engines did not indicate that they would share their technology with other licensees, and neither could they tap into the new developments of the other companies except by buying one of their products and taking it apart. And this seemed to be what was going on. GM's first generation rotary engines were all iron, inside and out, with single spark plugs. The press releases said that everything was going splendidly, but the engines were continuously being delayed as the engineers struggled with problems that many other companies had already worked out to their satisfaction. Most of their development problems seemed to be wrapped up in their attempts to build an engine that could be produced inexpensively and in huge quantities. They rejected proven materials in favor of less expensive ones only to have them fail. The long bolts that hold the layers of the engine together broke with maddening regularity. The iron rotor housings would not give up their heat fast enough, so they reluctantly turned to the more expensive aluminum. Attempts to save the cost of an external oil cooler were ill advised, as the rotors just got too hot without it. So for the prototype Corvette at least, the oil cooler re-appeared as a heat exchanger in the cooling system reservoir. Engineers also found that the expense of a second ignition system that they had hoped to do without was necessary if they were going to achieve any kind of fuel economy. The end result was an engine that looked remarkably like the one in Mazda's RX-2.

GM probably could have saved a lot of time and money if they had been a little less arrogant. Their failures were attributed to their attitude that said that they could go it alone in the development process where major companies like Curtiss-Wright and Daimler-Benz had already been spending millions in pure research. While it was true that GM's capacity for research and development was larger than that of any other auto maker in the world, the Wankel was still new technology and just assuming that they knew as much about it as anyone else turned out to be a costly mistake.

As it was, GM's effort was less research and more development. From the start, the emphasis of GM's rotary program was on ways to manufacture the engine. Instead of studying its unique thermodynamic characteristics, they built the engine as though it were a known property, and when problems inevitably arose, they lacked the body of knowledge for resolving those problems, a body of knowledge that only pure scientific research can produce. That research had already been done by Curtiss-Wright and other licensees, and had their license agreement been less exclusive, GM could have found answers to many of their problems in Curtiss-Wright's files.

In assuming that they already knew enough about the Wankel, GM also tried to make it fit their timetable. With each coming model year, engineers had always been expected to deliver their products on schedule, and the Wankel was expected to fall into place as well. The development engineers worked to a deadline, and in their haste to meet the deadlines, they had to cobble up patchwork solutions to problems rather than taking the time to study the problems and produce well thought out solutions.[1] The result was that rotary engine installations in experimental cars turned out to be plumber's nightmares even by R&D shop standards.

One effective solution that seemed to escape them was to copy Mazda's thermal reactor. GM's efforts to meet the EPA standards all centered on a large catalytic converter. The intent was to build the engine without the Mazda "albatross," a thermal reactor manifold made of cast iron and weighing about 20 pounds. The thermal reactor was the core of Mazda's emission control system and the central element of David Cole's research with the Curtiss-Wright engine. Publicly, GM passed the reactor off as a bulky piece of hot iron, but in a conversation with Rowland Berner, Dr. Craig Marks, a technical assistant to GM's engineering vice president, called the Mazda reactor a very impressive piece of work, with intricate sleeves and joints to allow it to expand without cracking under the heat. Marks said that he didn't know if GM could ever make one like it.[2]

With the benefit of hindsight, Marks also praised the Curtiss-Wright RC60 engine as a well developed machine, saying that after five years of work, GM still didn't know how to build that engine, and admitting that GM's approach was focused on manufacture and durability in an effort to get a rotary powered car on the road as quickly as possible.

Curtiss-Wright had the engine and the capacity to produce it, but no customers. American Motors and Chrysler were both in a position to buy engines from Curtiss-Wright, and would have done so in 1973 if they had to in order to build a car to compete with the GM rotary, but they were not going to make a move until General Motors did. As it turned out, had they bought engines from Curtiss-Wright at that time it would have been General Motors that would have been forced to rush an incomplete product into the market giving the lead to the smaller companies.

16

Rotary Motorcycles

Motorcycle manufacturers had also been watching the Wankel over the years, and many of them had obtained licenses to try their own hand at building a rotary engine. The Hercules had been the first. Marketed as a DKW for export from Germany, it used the air-cooled 20 horsepower engine built by Fichtel and Sachs. The engine was mounted with the fan in front, the engine's shaft running fore-aft in the frame with a six-speed transmission and shaft drive to the rear wheel. Early versions using the 20 horsepower engine had a top speed of 82 miles per hour while the later versions using a 32 horsepower engine could reach 93. It was not a successful motorcycle—only about 1800 were sold—but it did work and it did some groundbreaking for the motorcycle industry. All of the Wankel manufacturing equipment used by Hercules/ DKW was sold to the Norton Motorcycle Company of England in 1977, who were already working on their own rotary program while they were still Norton-Triumph-BSA.

Norton's first rotary cycle was the work of a development engineer named David Garside, an enthusiastic proponent of the rotary. It consisted of the same Fichtel and Sachs engine installed in a BSA 250 Starfire chassis. Garside was pleased with the performance but encountered engine cooling problems and was not interested in going to liquid cooling with all of the accompanying weight and complication. Bert Hopwood, a retired engine designer for Triumph, became interested in the project and together they worked up a twin rotor version with several times the cooling fin area of the original.

The method by which Sachs used the intake charge to cool the rotor was clever and effective, but the power loss incurred by heating the charge was greater than Garside could accept, so he altered the Sachs intake system to re-cool the charge after it passed through the rotor. The air was drawn into the engine from the front intake and passed through the inside of the rotor through a series of ports and channels in the housing and rotor. The air would pick up heat inside the rotor and then pass out of the engine into an intake plenum chamber. The air entered the chamber at a temperature of 100 degrees Centigrade and cooled to 75 degrees in the plenum. As the air passed through the carburetors it lost another 25 degrees to the evaporation of the fuel and entered the engine through peripheral intake ports at an acceptable 50 degrees Centigrade.[1]

The rotary Norton got its own frame and styling and went on sale. It was considered an ugly motorcycle by the entire industry; Cook Neilson in *Cycle* magazine called it "an alien lump of aluminum with arcane internals and an outward appearance only an air conditioner salesman could love." But its look could grow on you, its performance was undeniably outstanding, and in a country used to vertical twins, the lack of vibration was a relief. The rotary Norton made enough of an impression to keep the company going when all the other motorcycle divisions had long since closed. As late as 1988, Norton was still producing two rotary powered motorcycles, the air-cooled Classic and the liquid-cooled Police Commander.

Suzuki began work on the Wankel engine for motorcycles in 1970, and in 1975 they launched the RE-5. It was indeed an appropriate bike for the time as it was during the 1970s that the Japanese were getting away from the British designs that they had copied for so long and were really reaching out for anything new. The RE-5 was styled by Italian designer Georgetto Giugiaro who was responsible for a number of Ferraris and Alfa Romeos, but the grace of his car bodies did not carry over to motorcycles. The RE-5 had an ungainly appearance that began with the radiator, an accessory that people were not used to seeing on a motorcycle in 1975. Liquid cooled motorcycles were only beginning to appear, and Suzuki was doing some groundbreaking in that area as well with their liquid-cooled two stroke affectionately known as the "Water Buffalo."

The instruments were housed in a cylinder shaped like a Thermos bottle that lay atop the headlight nacelle and had a flip-up cover. The bodywork and frame were outfitted with circular and cylindrical devices and accessories

Figure 57. Four rotary powered motorcycles (clockwise from upper left): the Hercules W2000, BSA prototype, Van Veen, and Suzuki RE-5.

to echo the rotary theme, earning the early RE-5 models the nickname "Wurlitzer model" among collectors. Later production runs were a little more subtle in their styling treatment.

While it was the high power to weight ratio that made the rotary attractive for motorcycles, as it turned out, the RE-5 was neither powerful nor lightweight. The single rotor engine produced about 48 horsepower and the whole bike weighed in at 573 lbs. Performance was adequate, acceleration wasn't stunning, but high speed cruising was reported to be smooth and effortless.

Like the NSU Spider, the RE-5 was so heavy not because of the rotary engine, but because of the equipment needed to run it. The liquid cooling system added the weight of the radiator, the plumbing, and the coolant itself. The exhaust temperature was 300–400 degrees hotter than a conventional engine so the bike was equipped with a double walled exhaust system to contain the heat, adding yet more weight.

The Suzuki rotary engine was real progress. The all aluminum engine had peripheral port induction, a chrome plated trochoid housing, a four-piece self adjusting apex seal arrangement, and an extraordinarily complicated carburetor controlled by no fewer than five cables. Suzuki was so confident in their engine that they offered to replace engines at up to 12,000 miles. As it turned out, they did not have to replace many, as statistics eventually showed that instances of engine failure under warranty for the RE-5 were no greater than for conventional engines. Later owners reported getting 40,000–60,000 miles out of their engines before replacement.[2]

The Van Veen motorcycle consisted of a rotary engine installed in a Moto Guzi frame. The engines were Comotor KKM twin rotor liquid-cooled engines making 110 horsepower. The Van Veen was large at 620 lbs, expensive at £5000 and fast (top speed of over 130 mph). It was produced from 1976 to 1978.

Yamaha dabbled in rotary powered bikes with the prototype RZ201 under a license to produce Wankel engines owned by their subsidiary, Yanmar diesel. They built a 660cc liquid-cooled engine and showed the bike off at the 1973 Tokyo motor show, but it never went into production.

The Wankel was still showing various applications where fuel economy was not of particular concern. OMC (Outboard Marine Corporation) built a racing outboard motor that might have been quite successful if they could have gotten more seal life out of it. One witness to several outboard regattas where they were involved said that the rotaries took off and led the field every time for about two-thirds of the race, then as the seals deteriorated, they would start to slow down until the rest of the field passed them and left them behind. They would slow down more and more and might finish, but just barely.[3]

Arctic Cat made several models of snowmobiles with Fichtel and Sachs engines, and OMC built engines for Johnson and Evinrude snowmobiles. During 1974 and 1975, rotaries could be found in lawnmowers, water pumps and stationary generators. As with any unusual piece of machinery, there are still a few hard-core fans of the rotary snowmobiles cannibalizing some, to keep the last few going.

17

The RX-7

While other companies were dropping their rotary programs one by one, Mazda held on until it was the only major manufacturer of rotary engines left. The company had no choice, having invested too much in the rotary to back out. But Mazda now realized that it could not base its entire market on rotary engines. With the help of the banks, Mazda held itself together through 1975 and 1976 by cutting some 5,000 workers, mostly through attrition and retirement, hiring new management, and reorganizing its now cumbersome U.S. marketing organization. It shifted focus away from rotary powered cars and offered a line of conventional cars alongside the RX series. Small, front wheel drive econoboxes were very much in fashion in America, so Mazda put those in their showrooms for car-buyers who were too conservative for the rotary cars. Meanwhile, they continued to upgrade the RX series, offering the RX-3 and the more luxurious RX-4 in coupe, sedan and station wagon forms, the plush RX-5 Cosmo coupe, and even a rotary pickup truck. But sales continued to lag. Mazda's reorganization bought them the time they needed to improve their engine's gas mileage and reliability and introduce their comeback car in May of 1978, the RX-7.

The RX-7 had been anticipated since 1974 thanks to well placed rumors and carefully timed "leaks," but it was not seen until its proper introduction where it was presented next to the car it was most expected to compete with, a Porsche 924. A two-seat sport coupe, the RX-7 put the rotary in the per-

Figure 58. The original Mazda RX-7, introduced as a 1979 model (shown here in Japanese market form).

formance market where it belonged, and by the end of 1978, all of the other RX cars had been phased out leaving the RX-7 as the only rotary Mazda sold in America. It resembled the Porsche outside and inside as well, though the interior quality and finish of the Mazda was considerably better. The front was low and long, the hood nearly flat, and the windshield large and gracefully sloped. The roof was short, meeting with a long, sloped, unframed rear widow that opened to give access to a generous luggage compartment. Whether it was original or a copy, the shape of the RX-7 would be echoed in sports car design for at least a decade.

The interior was reminiscent of the Mercedes SL series. Through the leather covered steering wheel, the driver could see an instrument pod housing a centrally located tachometer, which doubled as a voltmeter before start-up, a temperature/fuel combination gauge on the left, and a speedometer on the right. The center console contained radio and heat/AC controls. In the two-seat coupe the rotary had a chance to show off its best qualities; its compact size, light weight and outstanding performance meant more here.

In many ways, the RX-7 was a very conventional car. The engine was mounted in front, coupled to a four or five speed or an automatic transmission, and drove the rear wheels. The suspension up front was McPherson strut, and in the rear it was a solid axle on coil springs. But the whole turned out to be far greater than the sum of the parts. Because the rotary was so light, Mazda was able to achieve near 50/50 weight distribution and a curb weight of 2350 lbs, helping to give the car very refined and balanced handling characteristics to complement the smooth and easy revving 100 horsepower engine. Acceleration was strong, 0–60 in 9.2 seconds when tested by *Motor Trend*. It ran the quarter mile in 16.7 seconds and had an observed top speed of over 120 mph.[1]

The 12-A rotary engine in the RX-7 was not the same engine that had given Mazda so many headaches in the early seventies. The rotor housings were still much the same, a chrome inner surface applied to a layer of steel that had been cast into the aluminum housing, but the apex seals had been changed from a carbon-aluminum alloy to an iron alloy with an edge crystallized to hardness by an electron beam. The corner seals were made of teflon and carbon fiber. Combustion chamber shape was changed from a symmetrical recess to a pear shaped recess that was deeper on the leading side of the rotor face. Sparkplug location was changed, as was the shape of the intake ports. All these subtle improvements and others brought the estimated gas mileage figures up to 19 MPG in the city and 29 on the highway, dramatically above the EPA's published mileage for the RX-2 of 10.4 in city driving.

The RX-7 received high praise from everyone who drove it as a competent sports car, well-balanced and easy to drive fast. It would have been considered a good car with a conventional engine, but with the unique characteristics of the rotary, it was an excellent car. Orders started rolling in. With Mazda hoping to sell the cars for under $7000, customers all over the country were dropping $1000 deposits on cars that had not yet been built, knowing they would have to wait six months or more for their car. Mazda execs were encouraged, but remained cautious. They knew that they had been caught

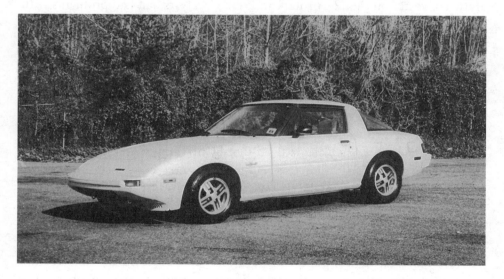

Figure 59. Example of a late first-generation RX-7 (the body-color bumper rub strips are nonstandard).

overconfident with their stepped-up production of the RX-2 and RX-3, and they didn't want to be caught again with a dock full of finished cars that they couldn't sell. So the RX-7 remained a sought after item with some dealers scalping new car prices and individuals selling used cars for more than the cost of a new one.

All through 1978 and 1979, RX-7s continued to sell well, amounting to a vindication for the Wankel rotary. Yamamoto had continued to tweak his designs and developments, and the RX-7s on the road were showing durability comparable to most piston engines and superior to some. It was now fair to expect 100,000 miles or more out of a well maintained RX-7 engine. As Yamamoto had said years before, it was just a question of finding the right materials to use together, and as materials science developed, so did the Mazda rotary.

American emissions regulations tightened up with every year, and with each model year change, the complications in the engine compartment got worse. As the manufacturers added device after device to clean up their act, the appearance of engine compartments began to reflect the desperation felt by the teams of researchers assigned the task. Raising the hood on each new model year was a daunting experience for mechanics trying to keep up with the technology as the number of vacuum lines, relays, switching valves and control units continued to increase. Mazda, which so far had been able to meet emissions standards without a catalyst, planned introduction of a catalytic converter on the 12-A rotary in 1980. Catalysts had had problems with durability when attached to a rotary, which was part of what frustrated GM during their research. The high hydrocarbons in the rotary's exhaust caused catalysts to overheat and burn out quickly. Mazda used a small version of their thermal reactor ahead of the catalyst to reduce the HC in the exhaust to manageable levels before the exhaust reached the catalyst. Another source of catalyst overheating was the tendency of a rotary to misfire when coasting or decelerating because of dilution of the intake charge with exhaust under high vacuum conditions. Mazda fixed that by first improving ignition, going from a three ground sparkplug to a four ground, and second installing a shutter valve that closed the intake passage to the rear rotor when the engine was decelerating and diverted it to the front rotor. Filling was thereby improved at the front so that there would be no misfiring there and fuel was shut off at the rear, preventing the passing of unburned HC because of poor combustion. In addition, air was pumped into the exhaust ports during deceleration to keep the thermal reactor going, the air being shifted to the mid-bed of the catalytic converter during normal running. Thus, the catalyst could survive life with a rotary long enough to pass the EPA's endurance tests and the engine could be tuned for better performance and fuel economy because the presence of the catalyst made excessively lean fuel mixtures unnecessary.

Experiments with supercharging had been going on for a while, and Mazda engineers liked a system they called TISC (Timed Injection with Supercharging). The system used a vane type air pump to build a supply of air at 30 psi which was fed into the engine via a rotating valve and an auxiliary port in the side cover. The valve was timed to engine rotation, so that the boosted air would only enter the engine during a certain part of the compression phase. Results were a 17 percent increase in torque at 1500 rpm and 13 percent at 3000.

It was turbocharging, however, that saw production, though not yet in the United States. Years before, the Cosmo name of sports car fame had been applied to a relatively large five passenger sedan that was driven by the 12A rotary of the RX-7. The Cosmo was only sold in Japan and turned into the guinea pig for Mazda's turbo marketing experiments. It was the Cosmo and not the RX-7 that got the turbo initially because the Japanese Transportation Ministry frowned on turbocharging sportscars for domestic sales. The plan was to test market the Cosmo turbo, then turn to building a turbocharged RX-7 for export if it went well.[2] In 1982, the Cosmo RE Turbo was the fastest car sold in Japan. It was clear that turbocharging would be a positive step for the RX-7 in America.

Another system in the works for improving gas mileage and overall efficiency on the non-turbocharged engines was the Variable Induction Port System (VIPS). It used a two stage throttle, and the secondary ports had two outlets in the housings. The primary inlets had their own ports in the center housings, and the secondaries had two each in the outer housings. Two of the secondary ports were opened by valves operated by exhaust gas pressure. The system gave the engine more flexibility over various speed ranges because it had, in effect, three induction port lengths to choose from for any given operating conditions.[3]

The VIPS system would eventually see production for the United States while the TISC would not. The VIPS would be used in the 1984 RX-7 GSL-SE with electronic fuel injection. The injection system was similar to the Bosch L Jetronic system that used intake air-flow and an exhaust oxygen sensor to determine the fuel mixture needs. Four injectors were used, two in the intake primaries and two in the secondary runners for added fuel on demand. The six intake ports on the engine were connected by long intake runners which doubled back over the top of the engine and came together at a two

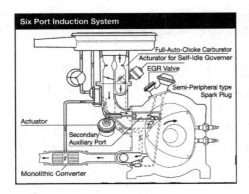
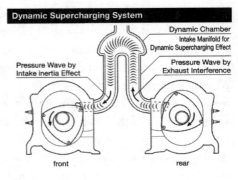

Figure 60. Mazda's six-port induction system (left) used auxiliary intake ports that were opened by devices activated by exhaust pressure. The dynamic supercharging system (right) made use of a pressure wave that occurs when an intake port is first uncovered. The pressure wave feeds back into the intake plenum and down the intake tract leading to a rotor that is on the cylinder filling part of its cycle.

story plenum chamber. The divisions in the plenum chamber made good use of the strong compression waves that are characteristic in the intake of a Wankel engine to achieve a ram effect between the rotor banks. Mazda called the effect "Dynamic Supercharging."

As one rotor face opened up to its intake port, a positive pressure wave created by remaining exhaust pressure would travel up the intake tract. The pressure wave entering the plenum chamber would then travel down an adjacent tube to a rotor chamber that was much farther along its intake cycle and assist in the chamber filling of that rotor. The lengths of the intake tracts were tuned to take best advantage of this effect at the most useful engine speeds. The system would be used on the 13B engine, the larger of the rotary engines that Mazda was producing at the time. Displacing 654cc per working chamber or 2.6 liters by the nearly universal formula of chamber displacement times two, times number of rotors, the VIPS equipped engine in the RX-7 made 135 HP at 6000 rpm and 133 lb ft of torque.

Mazda's engine naming scheme was based on the displacement of one working chamber times the number of rotors, which was how the Wankel engines were measured before tax agencies and race officials got involved. The 10A engine had a displacement of 491cc and two rotors: 491 times two is 982 or roughly one liter, indicated as 10; A designated the chronological version of the engine. First series, one liter engine: 10A. The 12A engine had chambers of 573cc times two rotors; or roughly 1.2 liters.

The 13B engine became the standard for many years, offering up its pieces in modular fashion for three and four rotor models. The 654cc sized rotor times two makes 1308cc; times three makes 1962cc in the 20B three rotor; and times four makes 2616 in the R26B four rotor Le Mans engine.

The RX-7 was offered with turbocharging for the Japanese market in the 1985 model year. Its engine control system was based on the Cosmo Turbo, but a few modifications had to be made to get the car to respond more quickly. The turbine blades were made smaller and their shape changed to draw more energy from the exhaust stream and get the turbine speed up from 100,000 rpm to 120,000.

Using a simpler fuel injection system and side housings with only two intake ports per rotor instead of three, the turbo delivered 140 horsepower SAE (165 as measured by the Japanese method). Quarter mile times were now under 15 seconds and top speed was an honest 140 miles per hour. It was just what the RX-7 needed to continue to compete with the other Japanese sportscars that were competing for its market like the Nissan 300ZX and the Toyota DOHC Celica.

The turbocharger did little to help the car off the line, however. It was still notoriously slow when driven at low engine speed shifting gears early. But above 2000 rpm the engine took off, quickly spinning up to its 7500 rpm redline.

The next generation RX-7 was launched in October 1985 for the 1986 model year. The new cars had the 13B engine with fuel injection and the Variable Induction Port System and the turbocharged cars gained an intercooler and a twin scroll turbocharger. The twin scroll turbo divided the exhaust into two passages and directed it onto different parts of the turbine according to different engine load and speed conditions. The process made the turbo more quickly adaptable to changes in engine speed. With the larger engine size, the twin scroll turbo, and the cooler intake charge provided by the intercooler, off-line performance was improved.

To make the whole package a little more attractive, handling was further improved by the addition of adjustable shock absorbers, which added a bit of user participation to the sport by permitting the driver to dial his suspension in the way he liked it. The brakes were made larger, limited slip differentials were made standard issue, and some cars were fitted with speed sensitive power steering. Later years saw the suspension become adjustable from the driver's seat and other additional options and appointments. But whatever happened to the package it was in, it was clear that Mazda had mastered the Wankel engine and made it work for them. Fuel consumption, oil consumption, engine durability and longevity were all within the range of the better high performance piston engines. Life expectancy of a well maintained 13B rotary was now easily as much as 150,000 miles.

Figure 61. The 13B rotary turbo engine.

So well developed was the Mazda rotary that for better performance, the engineers at Mazda started working again on projects to develop multi-rotor engines. In the early experimental days, the research department built a number of three and four rotor engines for testing, none of which saw the production lines. But several four rotor engines were now showing up in factory built prototypes at Le Mans, and in 1989, Mazda offered a four rotor competition engine.

Early in 1989, Mazda allowed automotive journalists a chance to drive the experimental three-rotor RX-7. No one went away unimpressed. It was favorably compared to V-12 engines because of its ultra smooth performance and flat, steady torque curve that enabled it to accelerate easily from 1000 rpm in fifth gear under full throttle.

The prototype three rotor, labeled the 20B-REW, was intended for eventual production, so it was based on the existing components of the 13-B engine already in the RX-7. The rotors and housings were the same as were the front and rear housings and one of the intermediate housings. Of course the eccentric shaft was different, with the lobes spaced 120 degrees apart instead of 180. And the additional intermediate housing, the one toward the front, was unique in that it had a main bearing in its center. The center main bearing had always been a puzzle because of the difficulty assembling one over the eccentric shaft. Most builders opted for a two rotor engine with no support in the center of the shaft, a design that worked fine in passenger car applications, though some racing engines experienced problems with shaft flex. In three or four rotor engines, that support has to be there. GM sidestepped the issue by simply bolting two engines together, but that made for a much bulkier unit. Curtiss-Wright built a two piece bearing support that had a split phasing gear on the outside. Mazda, however, built an eccentric shaft that tapered beyond the main bearing and had a removable eccentric lobe that was keyed to the shaft.

Mazda used a similar design with the four rotor engine, adding another rotor and housing with its own main bearing and removable eccentric at the rear of the engine.

The three rotor's output was 220 HP at 6500 rpm with 195 lb ft of torque at 3500 rpm compared to the two rotor's 146 HP and 138 lb ft of torque.

The three rotor engine never came to America in any form intended for street use. Mazda did use the three rotor with a turbocharger in a new full-sized home market luxury car called the Eunos Cosmo in 1990. The Eunos Cosmo was sold in Japan only, though for a while Mazda expressed interest in developing the Eunos line in America as a luxury arm of Mazda. The Eunos line would have been Mazda's answer to lines like Honda's Acura, Nissan's Infiniti and Toyota's Lexus.

Mazda also continued to research ways of getting more power out of the twin rotor engine. The turbocharged engine was good, but it was still universally a bit of a dud at low engine speeds.

Turbine blades were re-shaped to better take advantage of the exhaust gas velocity at low engine speeds (1500 rpm). Mazda also developed a system for manufacturing turbochargers that effectively eliminated the clearance between the turbine blade and the housing. The turbine housing had a sealing surface made of a special resin. The turbine blade was assembled to the housing and spun up to speed where the blade wore its shape into the resin. Thus each individual turbine was a perfect fit to its own housing. The new blade profile was designed to use the energy of the strong exhaust pulses that are characteristic of a rotary, and because of its smaller size, the inertia of the turbine was reduced which enhanced the ability of the turbine to adjust quickly to changes in load. But a small turbine has little effect on high speed output, so Mazda added another turbo, to engage sequentially to increase boost above 1500 rpm.

The exhaust stream ran to both turbochargers, but a control valve was installed in the passage to the larger turbine. Another control valve was placed in the compressor passage of the larger compressor to prevent boost pressure from spilling back down through the secondary turbocharger. The control valves were operated by exhaust pressure and boost pressure and fine tuned by a computer control system to bring on the maximum boost according to engine load and speed. So that the large compressor would not have to spin up from idle the instant it was called for, a clever system routed exhaust from the wastegate of the small turbo to the larger one to get it going. Once the control valves opened, bringing the larger turbo into play, the turbine was already spinning at 80,000 rpm. Test drivers noticed a slight falling off of torque during transition

Figure 62. The third generation RX-7, introduced for 1993.

to the secondary turbocharger, but it was small enough to cause little concern. The sequential turbo arrangement increased available torque at 1500 rpm by 36 percent. Time required to reach maximum boost pressure was reduced by 43 percent. And time to reach maximum acceleration was reduced by 50 percent.

In Japan, the sequential turbo was sold on the Cosmo with the three rotor engine, making a 300 HP powerplant for the 2+2 coupe. For America, the sequential turbo was put on the new 1993 third generation RX-7.

The latest edition of the RX-7 was sold in the USA in 1993, 1994 and 1995. Despite aggressive new styling, light weight and an enthusiastic reception in the automotive press, sales were dropping off. Troubles in the Japanese economy were driving up the price of the cars so

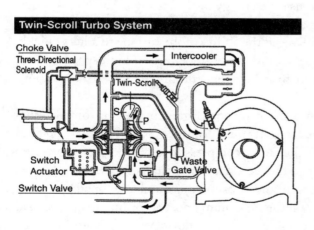

Figure 63. Mazda's twin scroll turbo system divided the exhaust going into the turbine into two tracts, one of which operated only at high speeds. This maintained high exhaust velocity and therefore high turbo speed, reducing turbo lag.

that they were no longer affordable sports cars in the United States but increasingly high priced exotics. (The same was true of two of the RX-7's chief Japanese competitors, the Nissan 300Zx and Toyota Supra, both of which failed in the U.S. marketplace around the same time.) So Mazda finally pulled the RX-7 from the U.S. market in favor of promoting its family vans, sedans and small pickup trucks as well as the successful non-rotary sports car the MX-5 Miata. The RX-7 was still sold in Japan and Australia for a few years, then in 1999 it became available only in Japan.

18

Rotaries in Racing

Not long after the RX-2s and RX-3s hit the market, amateur and professional racers discovered that they had potential on the race tracks. In 1973, the International Motor Sport Association (IMSA) sanctioned a class called Baby Grand Sedan. An article written by Patrick Bedard, "Rotary Racer and Piston Politics," in April 1974 described how a team of amateur racers from *Car and Driver* magazine prepared a new RX-2 to Baby Grand specifications and entered the car in five races. Enduring some development problems, more related to brakes and chassis than to engine problems, they won two races out of the five and demonstrated the ability of the Wankel racer to dominate the field. At the end of the season, however, IMSA changed the rules regulating allowable modifications to the Mazda, rendering it uncompetitive in the opinion of the *Car and Driver* team.

The formulas for calculating displacement came into dispute more than once. The displacement of a piston engine is figured by multiplying the volume of one cylinder by the number of cylinders. If the Wankel's displacement were figured according to the same type of formula as a piston engine, it would be a matter of multiplying the swept volume of a single chamber by the number of rotors. By this formula, the rotary far outstrips the performance of a piston engine. Taking into consideration that a single-rotor engine produces one power stroke per revolution of the output shaft, as opposed to one power stroke per two revolutions for a single cylinder four-stroke piston engine, the sanctioning bodies adopted the formula that most of the rest of the rotarians have: that of multiplying the chamber displacement by two, then by the number of rotors. Naturally those who would race rotaries would prefer the former, as it would place the engine among piston engines of smaller displacement and give them a tremendous power advantage in a given class. Nevertheless there was still much interest in the rotary's potential for racing.

The *Car and Driver* team came away from their effort convinced that even in the larger displacement class, the rotary was actually better suited for amateur racing than conventional piston engines. They went on to qualify that this conclusion applied only to classes based on production engines and not on purpose built racing engines. The 1973 rules under which they ran permitted only the use of stock rotors and allowed no port enlargement at the manifold face and no enlargement of the carburetor throttles. The *Car and Driver* team's engine produced about 218 horsepower at 8400 rpm and made 140 lb-ft of torque at 6000 rpm. These totals were lower than the fastest car in the competition, but it was where and how the power came on that made the difference. The power of a piston engine normally reaches its peak below redline, then falls off fairly quickly as the revolutions rise, but the Mazda engine continued to put out, with the power falling off by only 5 percent at 9000 rpm. The superior low end of the piston engines gave them a quicker jump out of the corners, but on the longer tracks, the Mazdas could recover the distance and on the long straightaways like Daytona or Road Atlanta, they had about five miles per hour more in top speed.

In amateur racing the cost of maintaining a race car becomes important. The Mazda was practically maintenance free for the season. As long as it had an adequate supply of fresh oil and coolant, it needed little upkeep, even enduring over-revs of missed shifts. Allowing it to overheat, though, meant a disaster. Most owners didn't want to tackle the complications of engine overhaul, particularly when the housings were distorted by excessive heat, so cooling system problems often meant engine replacement.

There were also problems involved in dealing with teardowns for technical inspection. The *Car and Driver* team was once subjected to a teardown by officials to verify that the engine was running with stock rotors. Instead of a simple cylinder head removal, the front and rear housings had to be removed to reveal the rotors and, as these were held in place by bolts that ran the length of the engine, all the tension was relieved by their removal. At that point, it was not just a matter of re-installing the end housings; the entire engine had to be dismantled and all seals between housings replaced before it could go back together. The officials found that the rotors were stock.

The IMSA rule changes of 1974 effectively put the Mazda sedans out of the running by prohibiting any modification to the engine ports. Even though port enlargement at the manifold face was prohibited before, builders were able to make significant gains by enlarging the ports on the face of the side housings, thereby increasing their opening area and their opening time. The new rules effectively reduced the engine's output to a potential of 135 horsepower. *Car and Driver* expressed the opinion that the new rule was a political move on the part of IMSA ownership to limit the potential of the Wankels. They felt that the leadership of IMSA was not prepared to see a strange new engine come out of nowhere and win the BF Goodrich Challenge races. Rather they thought that seeing American built cars like Pintos and Gremlins winning would be more appropriate for the venue.

In classes sanctioned by the SCCA, the Mazdas could be raced in several different trims. In most cases, it was the R100 engine that was eligible for the smaller sedan classes where the car could be at the top of the class. The RX-3, because of its larger displacement, was ineligible for the smaller classes and ended up lumped in with cars with much larger engines like the Corvette and Porsche 911. But in GT racing, sufficient modification was allowed that a determined racer with the money to spend could obtain such factory racing pieces as a stainless steel exhaust system and peripheral port rotor housings that were offered by Mazda. Thus equipped, sufficient horsepower could be achieved making the cars competitive, but only just.[1]

But the RX-7 was another story. The RX-7s were the most successful race-car ever. In IMSA racing the RX-7 won more races than any other model car. In GTO class, an RX-7 won the 24 hours of Daytona ten years in a row. From 1980 to 1990, the RX-7 won ten GTU manufacturers championships. In the SCCA, cars with Mazda engines have won over 100 amateur titles.

In the eastern United States, Mazda rotaries became popular with hill climb racers. Relieved of the bulk of its external equipment and emission controls, the small engine made a neat and powerful package that could be installed in practically anything. Mazda engines could be found under the hood of any number of British sports cars. But their performance was most impressive when they were installed in ultralight Formula Ford or one-off homebuilt chassis. Mazda-powered hill climb "specials" were nearly unbeatable for almost ten years running.

During the 1990s, the Formula Mazda racing series was launched by a group calling themselves NASA, for National Auto Sport Association. Inspired by the Formula Ford and Club Ford cars, the Formula Mazda is an open wheeled race car powered by a standard Mazda 13B engine. The Formula

Mazda is known as a spec series. Most of the features of the car are standardized, and the engines are sealed to prevent modification. Modifications of tire sizes, shock absorbers, and the rear wings are permitted. Ideally the competition is balanced this way and the racing becomes a test of the driver's skill rather than the capacity of his wallet. Likewise NASA runs a pro RX-7 series. It is also a spec series for 1979 to 1985 RX-7s.

Outside the spec series, the RX engines lent themselves well to the amateur tuner. Numerous carburetion and exhaust setups were available for the people who could not afford the peripheral port housings. And those same people loved to experiment with changing the shape of the intake ports in the side housings, which the SCCA permitted. Many of their attempts did more harm than good, but every now and then, someone would stumble on the right combination and be well rewarded by the performance.

But long before the madness began among amateurs, Andy Granatelli, a well known race car owner and engine oil additive tycoon, was reported to have approached Curtiss-Wright in 1968 about purchasing several four-rotor Wankels for his own use in racing at Indianapolis. It was a plan to follow up his turbine race cars which he had campaigned at Indy, finally winning with Mario Andretti driving. The ultra-conservative management at Curtiss-Wright at that time did not recognize the value of having the new engine introduced to America in such a venue, and the deal never went through. In failing to complete the deal, they missed a tremendous chance. Had Granatelli been able to appear or even win at Indianapolis with a Wankel powered car, the resulting publicity might have changed the way the public and the major American auto manufacturers viewed the upstart new engine.[2]

Mazda saw in racing, particularly in the 24 hours of Le Mans, an excellent opportunity to vindicate the rotary of many of its published faults. Simply finishing the race is a badge of honor for a manufacturer; to win, especially for an underdog can be world shaking. So Mazda participated from the early days of its rotary program. In 1970, they supplied a 10A engine to a private Belgian team who installed it in a Chevron B16 race car and entered it in Le Mans. The car lasted only four hours because of a broken cooling hose. Their next entry was in 1973 with a 12A engine in a Japanese Sigma race car. That car dropped out after 11 hours due to electrical system problems. The next Sigma entry in 1974 was still going after 24 hours and received a checkered flag, but did not have enough laps to qualify.

In 1975 a French team entered a Mazda S124 A but did not finish. In 1979, Mazda Auto Tokyo entered in an RX-7/252I, but barely got started before having to drop out. The first Mazda rotary to finish the 24 Hours of

The Mazda R26B competition four rotor engine, victorious at LeMans in 1991.

Le Mans was in 1980, when an American team entered an RX-7 and finished twenty-first overall.

Mazda Auto Tokyo continued their entries in 1981, dropping out because of gearbox problems. In 1982 they entered two RX7 254s in GTX, one of which finished sixth in class, fourteenth overall. In 1983 they moved their focus to the new Group C Junior category and built two mid-engine sports prototype cars which they labeled the 717C. The two cars finished first and second in class and twelfth and eighteenth overall.

Mazda Auto Tokyo changed the name of their racing department to Mazda Speed and became the focal point for Mazda's racing activity. They redesigned the 717C into the 727C and also had two Laura T616 cars prepared by the BF Goodrich team. All four cars were entered in 1984, and all four finished. The Lauras finished first and third in class, tenth and twelfth overall. The 727Cs finished fourth and sixth in class, fifteenth and twentieth overall.

The 1985 entries from Mazda Speed were two 737Cs, which were upgrades of the 727s. They finished third and sixth in class, nineteenth and twenty-fourth overall, after suffering transmission problems. In 1986, Mazda entered in the GTP class with two new 757s equipped with the new three rotor 13G engine, both dropping out with driveshaft problems. Next year their luck was better and one of the 757s won the GTP category, placing seventh overall.

The 1988 entries were two newly developed 767s with new 13J four rotor engines, plus one 757. The 767s finished in seventeenth and nineteenth overall, not competing well because of exhaust manifold cracking. The 757 finished fifteenth overall, suffering brake problems.

In 1989 Mazda entered two 767Bs and one 767. Two cars crashed during qualifying, but the crews were able to repair them so that all three cars could start and finish. They finished first, second and third in GTP, and seventh, ninth and twelfth place overall. The following year saw again two new cars, 787s with the new four rotor R26B engine, and one 767B. The 767 won

Figure 65. The LeMans winning 787B of 1991.

the GTP class, placing twentieth overall, but the 787s had to drop out because of excessive fuel consumption.

Mazda's final triumph was in 1991. According to race officials, rotary engines would be disqualified next year so this was Mazda's last chance for a first place finish. They entered three cars, an old 787 and two new 787Bs. The fuel consumption problems had been worked out in the R26B engine and the 787's carbon fiber body had been strengthened in the 787B. The car weighed 1831 lbs and the four rotor engine produced 700 horsepower. After 12 hours of racing, the 787B number 55 made it into third place and ran in the front pack for another nine hours before moving into the lead spot while Mercedes was in the pits. Mazda was able to hang on to the lead for the rest of the race and at the 24 hour mark, the 787Bs finished first and sixth place overall.

The disqualification of the rotaries did not happen, and Mazdas were able to compete in subsequent years. But the factory did not pour as much effort into the race as they had up until the win in 1991. Mazda fans are still hopeful that the company management will again turn to racing to promote rotary cars.

19

Current and Future Production

From 1957 to 2000, Wankel's rotary underwent 43 years of development, a similar time span to that enjoyed by the reciprocating gasoline engine that it was meant to replace when the rotary was first conceived. It never actually proved superior in every respect, the way many of its backers had claimed, but it most certainly had a chance to show that it had its niche. Mazda-backed racing, particularly their win at Le Mans, went a long way to show that the rotary was a contender on even ground with the best the automotive industry had to offer. Even other manufacturers of rotary engines cite Mazda's Le Mans win as evidence of the rotary engine's durability.

After years of developing the rotary for aircraft use, Curtiss-Wright sold its whole Wankel program to Deere and Co., aka John Deere, in 1984 for a down payment of only $2 million with subsequent installments. Despite all the time and money spent on development, and the fact that they had the know-how to build some of the best rotaries in the world, Curtiss-Wright had never been able to find a market for its engines. Deere began developing a rotary aircraft engine built on Curtiss-Wright's work in collaboration with Lycoming until Lycoming pulled the plug in 1987 because of a slump in the aircraft industry. Deere also built on the work that Curtiss-Wright had done on heavy fuel engines, developing from the DISC (Direct Injected Stratified

Charge) technology what they called the SCORE (Stratified Charge Omnivorous Rotary Engine) for possible military vehicle and heavy equipment applications. The rotary's non-particular appetite makes it a good candidate for machinery that may be required to run on low grade fuels depending on availability. The possible military applications are obvious. A vehicle or stationary generator engine used on an airbase can use jet fuel, while a SCORE rotary on a diesel ship can burn diesel fuel. Land vehicles used in combat operations can use any fuel supply that is available including captured fuel supplies of gasoline or kerosene.

Deere and Company had several promising ventures lined up with the government that never gelled. One Marine Corps contract had them building seven 750 horsepower engines for installation and testing in a new amphibious assault vehicle. Under another contract with the Navy they built and installed a SCORE 580 series 650 horsepower engine in a 65 foot boat for testing and evaluation of its marine performance. The Air Force was interested in SCORE engines for portable generator sets, and the designers of the Abrams tank were looking at a rotary engine for their auxiliary power generator to save enough space to make room for a new automatic loader.

It all seemed very promising for a while, but as Curtiss-Wright had known all too well, where government contracts are involved, a company can have the financial rug pulled out from under a project at a moment's notice. That happened to John Deere, and in 1991 they sold they whole rotary program to a new company formed to develop and market rotary engines.

Rotary Power International (RPI) bought the rotary program from Deere and Company in 1991, acquiring with it the sum developmental experience amassed by Curtiss-Wright and John Deere over 32 years and at a cost of over $200 million. In addition they obtained the services of Charles Jones, Bill Figart and a number of other engineers and employees who had been with the rotary from its beginnings at Curtiss-Wright. Most of the products that John Deere had been working on were picked up by RPI, which continued to develop them and to seek out new markets.

Apart from the military and marine applications that Deere had focused on, RPI has become involved in a pilot project with a biomass gasification company to construct a generating plant powered by their engines running on gas generated from agricultural wastes. RPI claims that the rotary engine is especially well suited to using biomass gases because of its ability to run on unusually lean mixtures.

At this writing, RPI planned to offer three families of engines built around three different rotor sizes. The 70 series has a single rotor displacement

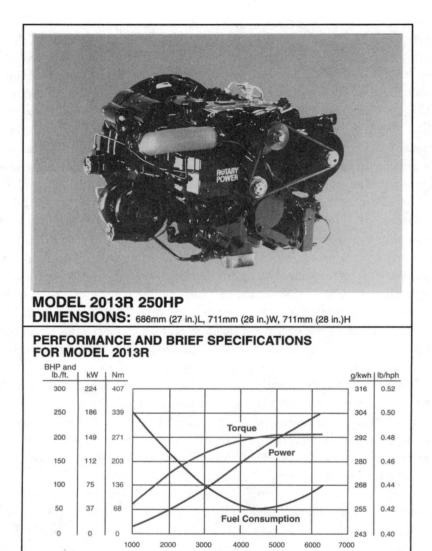

MODEL 2013R 250HP
DIMENSIONS: 686mm (27 in.)L, 711mm (28 in.)W, 711mm (28 in.)H

PERFORMANCE AND BRIEF SPECIFICATIONS FOR MODEL 2013R

BHP and lb./ft.	kW	Nm		g/kwh	lb/hph
300	224	407		316	0.52
250	186	339		304	0.50
200	149	271	Torque	292	0.48
150	112	203	Power	280	0.46
100	75	136		268	0.44
50	37	68		255	0.42
0	0	0	Fuel Consumption	243	0.40

Engine Speed – RPM (1000 2000 3000 4000 5000 6000 7000)

• For multi-rotor versions, power and torque increase in proportion to the number of rotors. Specific fuel consumption is the same.

2-rotor engine
Displacement – 1.3L (80 in.³)
Weight – 159 kg (350 lb.) Dry
Rated power – 186 kW (250hp)
Rated speed – 6250 rpm
Injection – direct
Ignition – spark

Fuel – multiple fuel use (includes combat gasoline, JP-5, JP-8, Jet A, No. 1 and No. 2 diesel fuel)

Rotation – counterclockwise when viewed from flywheel end of engine

Figure 66. One of a number of general purpose engines to be offered by Rotary Power International.

of .7 liters or 40 CI, and can be built in sizes up to four rotors, 2.6 liters, 320 HP. The 170 series is built around a rotor size of 1.7 liters and may be as big as 6 rotors, 10.2 liters, 630 HP. The largest engines, the 580 series, will be built around a 5.8 liter rotor and are planned in up to a six rotor size, 34.7 liters, 2250 HP.

Wankel GmbH is still in business, and as of year 2001 they produce aircraft engines in sizes ranging from 407cc and 35 HP to 1628 cc and 150 HP. They have heavy fuel (diesel or kerosene) engines and also build air compressors and superchargers.

Mazda of course has its corporate identity still wrapped up in the rotary. As of year 2001, it is the only automobile company still owning the rights to produce and sell Wankel rotary engines. The company has confidence in its ability to adapt the rotary to future needs as the regulatory and economic environments change. The American and Japanese governments keep raising the bar with emission regulations, but the Mazda engineers know how the engine works like no one else in the world and they seem to be able to meet the continuing challenge. Although the rotary nearly destroyed Mazda in the early 1970s as the company was almost dragged under by mounting debt and plummeting sales, it is likely that had they not invested in the rotary technology, Mazda would have been absorbed by one of the giant Japanese car makers. As it was, they maintained their identity and eventually their solvency.

As part of their development for future markets, in 1991 Mazda displayed a hydrogen powered rotary engine at the Tokyo Motor Show. Hydrogen is an excellent motor fuel because it produces no carbon monoxide, no carbon dioxide, and no hydrocarbon emissions at all. Its chief drawback is that it is more difficult to store safely than gasoline. Probably the most innovative part of this package was not the engine, but the hydrogen storage system. Rather than keeping the fuel in liquid form in a cryogenic tank, Mazda stored the hydrogen in a metal hydride tank which releases the gas slowly as the tank is heated by the engine's coolant. To refuel the tank, the tank is cooled by an external water source while the fresh hydrogen is piped in. The hydrogen atoms are contained as they occupy space within the crystal lattice of the metal atoms. When heated again the hydrogen is again liberated.

Mazda engineers claim that the rotary is better suited than a conventional piston engine to burning hydrogen. Because the combustion cycle is slower, there is more time for the fuel and air to mix before it is ignited. Additionally, the Mazda engine lacks an exhaust valve, which on conventional engines run on hydrogen glows red hot during operation and tends to ignite the fuel mixture prematurely. The lack of an exhaust valve and the relatively cool combustion chamber walls of the rotary prevent this problem.

The hydrogen powered engine, installed in a concept car, was used alongside a motor-generator unit that served as a starter and alternator, and supplemented the torque of the engine to assist in rapid acceleration. But for real world road testing, hydrogen powered rotaries were fitted to Mazda Miatas using a conventional drivetrain. The system makes good sense. Probably the biggest barrier to hydrogen powered vehicles is the lack of infrastructure for regular refueling. But once the market is there, the structure will surely develop quickly and Mazda plans to have hydrogen powered cars working when the time is right for ultra-low emission vehicles.[1]

America has not seen any rotary cars since Mazda stopped shipping in RX-7s, but rotary lovers are hopeful. In 1999 at the Tokyo Auto Show, Mazda introduced the RX-Evolv, a concept car to represent their next generation of rotary powered cars. The RX-Evolv has a very striking shape, low and sleek with rounded corners like the cars of the future as envisioned by the artists of the 1930s, with the wheels well out toward the corners of the car. The long wheelbase on a relatively short car lends enough space for the body's most surprising feature, four doors. The rear doors open "suicide style," hinged at the rear like those of the 1961–1967 Lincoln Continental to provide access to fairly spacious back seats with modern features like built in baby seats. Mazda refers to the RX-Evolv as a family sports car.

Figure 67. Design studies of the RX-EVOLV.

The new car is equipped with control features borrowed from racing and mounted on the steering wheel. The transmission is a six speed auto shift manual. There is no clutch pedal, and the driver can select automatic shifting controlled electronically, or can shift by paddles mounted on the steering wheel like a Formula One car. There is also an active cornering brake function controlled from the steering wheel that can automatically apply the brakes to individual wheels to enhance cornering capabilities.

The RX-Evolv is powered by Mazda's new Renesis engine, a development of the MSP-RE engine that powered a previous concept car, the RX-01, and was in turn a derivation of the 13 REW that powered the twin turbo RX-7. MSP stands for multi side ports, the largest change in the engine being the movement of the exhaust ports from the periphery of the housing to the side housings below the intakes. This change eliminates the overlap period when both ports are uncovered and makes it possible to increase the size of the intakes resulting in increased power output and efficiency. Mazda says that its engineers tried the side intake-exhaust configuration during earlier days of development, but the sealing technology of the time was not up to it. New developments however made it possible to maintain the seal and employ the breathing improvements of the side port layout. The side port layout is complemented by Mazda's variable length induction system that uses tuned induction tracts that are selected by throttle valves to optimize the tract length for engine speed and load.

The rotors in the Renesis have been lightened, and as a result, the maximum revolution limit has been raised to 10,000 rpm. Maximum power is found further up the scale at 9000 rpm instead of 6500. These kinds of engine speeds are unusual in a street machine; most conventional sports cars are still limited to 7000 rpm or less. Mazda's version of the rotary is coming closer to becoming the race horse that Wankel had envisioned rather than the cart horse that he had labeled it.

Figure 68. Cutaway view of the Renesis engine.

With the hydrogen cars and the RX-Evolv, Mazda has demonstrated itsr commitment to the rotary engine for the future. Even though they now have a full line of conventional cars, the rotary itself has become a major part of the company's identity. The Mazda name has become synonymous with the rotary engine and most people who are well acquainted with Mazda have no idea who Felix Wankel was or what the possible connection could be.

There were many "ifs" in the story of the Wankel engine. If General Motors had not tried to go it alone but instead taken a license that gave them access to Curtiss-Wright's technology, they could have built a much more durable unit that might have gone into production. If the other American manufacturers had chosen to take a leading position and bought engines from Curtiss-Wright, they might have opened a new market in the United States for themselves. If oil prices hadn't gone up at almost exactly the same time that the EPA started publishing gas mileage figures, Americans' interest in the rotary might have remained strong enough to inspire U.S. car companies to build rotary-powered cars. If things had gone just a little differently, the Wankel might have found much more widespread use in the world.

As it is, it has done well. It made its inventor and many other people very rich, and made a niche for itself in markets where high power to weight ratios are important. The piston engine has also come a long way in the last 40 years, and current engines are amazingly efficient, and far more durable than they were in the day of the rotary's conception, but the Wankel is still getting better. Perhaps as materials science advances, and companies like Wankel GmbH, Mazda and RPI continue to work on it, the rotary will someday be able to match the efficiency of the piston engine.

But Wankel's engine was not all about money. He invented his engine because it was a piece of a puzzle that he had always wanted to solve. No doubt, had the prospects of outrageous wealth not been attached to the outrageous new engine, it would likely have died in the cradle at NSU. But the businessmen who initially took a chance on it were mostly engineers at heart. Men like Hurley at Curtiss-Wright, von Heydekampf at NSU, Mitsuda and Yamamoto at Mazda and Cole at General Motors fell in love with the concept and did what they could to make it work, often at their own peril. The concept of a totally new engine with years of development ahead cannot make it through the boardroom of a rigidly conservative company. Even the engineers themselves tend to be deeply conservative by nature. There has to be a gambler at the wheel, someone who can see elegance in a concept and want to develop it simply for its own sake and forget about the cost. Fortunately there are still a few around, nurturing new thoughts and keeping things interesting.

Notes

Chapter 1

1. Crow, James T. "Stroke of Genius." *Road & Track*, August 1983, p. 164.

Chapter 3

1. Faith, Nicholas. *Wankel: The Curious Story Behind the Revolutionary Rotary Engine.* New York: Stein and Day, 1975, pp. 31–33.
2. Froede, Walter. "NSU Wankel Rotating Combustion Engine." *SAE Transactions* vol. 69 (1961), pp. 179–193.
3. Norbye, Jan P. *The Wankel Engine: Design, Development, Applications.* Radnor, PA: Chilton, 1971, pp. 99–101.
4. Faith. *Wankel: The Curious Story*, p. 45.
5. Fisher, Joachim. "I Drove the Wankel-Engine Car at 90 MPH!" *Popular Science* 116 (December 1961), pp. 72–73.

Chapter 4

1. Bentele, Max. *Engine Revolutions: The Autobiography of Max Bentele.* Warrendale, PA: Society of Automotive Engineers, 1991.
2. *Ibid.*, p. 152.

3. *Ibid.*, p. 154.
4. Norbye, *Wankel Engine*, p. 213.
5. *Ibid.*, p. 217.
6. Norbye, Jan. "Test Drive of US Car with a Rotating Combustion Engine." *Popular Science*, April 1966, pp. 102–107.
7. Norbye, *Wankel Engine*, pp. 239–241.

Chapter 5

1. Faith, *Wankel: The Curious Story*, p. 129.
2. Yamaguchi, Jack. "Profile: Kenichi Yamamoto." *Road & Track* 30 (July 1979), pp. 22+.
3. Faith, *Wankel: The Curious Story*, pp. 129, 130.
4. Norbye, *Wankel Engine*, pp. 258, 259.
5. Yamamoto, Kenichi, and Takashi Kuroda. "Toyo Kogyo's Research and Development on Major Rotary Engine Problems" *SAE Transactions.* Paper #700079 for SAE meeting of January 1970.
6. Ansdale, R.F. "Wankel Progress." *Motor Trend*, February 1966, pp. 29+.
7. Martin, "The Company That Makes the Mazda," p. 104–106+.
8. Faith, *Wankel: The Curious Story*, pp. 189, 190.

Chapter 6

1. "The Rotary Engine Gets on the Road." *Business Week*, April 3 1965, p. 8.
2. David Scott. "Power Without Pistons." *Popular Science* 186 (January 1965), pp. 60–63.
3. "The Rotary Engine Gets on the Road," p. 10.
4. *Ibid.*
5. Ansdale, R.F. "Wankel Progress." *Motor Trend*, February 1966, pp. 29–30.

Chapter 7

1. Ansdale, R. F. "Air Cooled Wankel Engine." *Automobile Engineer*, August 1965, pp. 354–356.

Chapter 8

1. Faith, *Wankel: The Curious Story.*
2. Norbye, *Wankel Engine*, p. 423.
3. Norbye, "Citroen Goes All Out," pp. 57, 58.

Chapter 9

1. Faith, *Wankel: The Curious Story*, pp. 97–98.
2. Norbye, *The Wankel Engine*, p. 297.
3. Frere, Paul. "Mercedes-Benz C111." *Road & Track*, January 2001, p. 85.

Chapter 10

1. Faith, *Wankel: The Curious Story*, p. 145.
2. "Rolls-Royce Two Stage Rotary Engine." *Automobile Engineer*, February 1971, pp. 30–32.
3. Faith, *Wankel: The Curious Story*, p. 146.

Chapter 11

1. Boffy, Phillip M. "Nixon's Panel Reports on the Environment." *Science* 163 (February 7, 1969), p. 549.
2. "Nixon Proposes NOAA and EPA." *Science* 169 (July 17, 1970), p. 266.
3. "A Costly Order to Auto Makers: Clean Up by 1975." *U.S. News and World Report*, May 22, 1972, p. 61.

Chapter 12

1. Faith, *Wankel: The Curious Story*, pp. 169–170.
2. "Wangle Yourself a Wankel." *Forbes*, December 15, 1972, pp. 25.
3. *Ibid.*
4. "Wankel," *Motor Trend*, November 1972, p. 72.
5. "Wangle Yourself a Wankel." *Forbes*, December 15, 1972, pp. 24–27.
6. *Ibid.*
7. Wyss, Wally. "The '75 Vega Rotary." *Motor Trend*, July 1973, pp. 50+.
8. Ludvigsen, Karl. "Scoop of the Year!" *Motor Trend*, November 1973, pp. 57–60.

Chapter 13

1. "Wangle Yourself a Wankel," pp. 26–27.
2. Smith, Steve. "Road Test: Mazda's RX2." *Motor Trend*, November 1972, p. 67.
3. Faith, *Wankel: The Curious Story*, pp. 196–199.
4. "The Rotary Turnabout," *Forbes*, March 1, 1975, p. 46.

Chapter 14

1. Faith, *Wankel: The Curious Story*, p. 95.
2. Faith, *Wankel: The Curious Story*, pp. 111–114.
3. Burck, Charles. "A Car That May Re-Shape the Industry's Future." *Fortune*, July 1972, p. 79.

Chapter 15

1. Ludvigsen, Karl. "GM's Wankel: The $700 Million Miscalculation." *Motor Trend*, March 1975, p. 53.
2. Ludvigsen, Karl. "Out of Round, Round and Round the Rotary Round Table," *Motor Trend*, April 1976, p. 14.

Chapter 16

1. Neilson, Cook. "Impression: Triumph Rotary," *Cycle*, November 1974, pp. 29–33.
2. Ross, Brent. "Suzuki RE5 Rotary." *Cycle*, February 1988, pp. 55–59.
3. Quote from eyewitness, Pete McHenry.

Chapter 17

1. Nerpal, Chuck. "Mazda RX-7." *Motor Trend*, May 1978, pp. 73–77.
2. Ishiwatara, Yasushi. "Mazda Cosmo Turbo GT." *Car and Driver*, June 1983, p. 25.
3. Sherman, Don. "Technical Highlights: Rotary Engine Refinement." *Car and Driver*, January 1981, p. 32.

Chapter 18

1. Bedard, Patrick. "Rotary Racer and Piston Politics." *Car and Driver*, April 1974, pp. 68–74.
2. Yates, Brock. "The New Little Engine That Couldn't." *Sports Illustrated*, April 16, 1973, pp. 79–81.

Chapter 19

1. Normille, Dennis. "Mazda's Hydrogen Miata." *Popular Science*, February 1993, p. 53.

Index